The Mystery of Reality

*To Bernard and Pauline,
With love and best wishes,
Chris.*

The Mystery of Reality

*With its Implications for Love, Religious Faith
and the Courage to be Oneself*

Christopher G. Smith

Copyright © 2013 Christopher G. Smith

The moral right of the author has been asserted.

Apart from any fair dealing for the purposes of research or private study, or criticism or review, as permitted under the Copyright, Designs and Patents Act 1988, this publication may only be reproduced, stored or transmitted, in any form or by any means, with the prior permission in writing of the publishers, or in the case of reprographic reproduction in accordance with the terms of licences issued by the Copyright Licensing Agency. Enquiries concerning reproduction outside those terms should be sent to the publishers.

Matador
9 Priory Business Park,
Wistow Road, Kibworth Beauchamp,
Leicestershire. LE8 0RX
Tel: (+44) 116 279 2299
Fax: (+44) 116 279 2277
Email: books@troubador.co.uk
Web: www.troubador.co.uk/matador

ISBN 978 1780883 359

British Library Cataloguing in Publication Data.
A catalogue record for this book is available from the British Library.

Typeset by Troubador Publishing Ltd, Leicester, UK

Matador is an imprint of Troubador Publishing Ltd

Printed and bound in the UK by TJ International, Padstow, Cornwall

*To my parents, Doris and George,
for their precious gift of love.*

CONTENTS

Preface	xi
Acknowledgements	xviii
How to Read this Book	xix

Chapter 1. The End of Faith?	**1**
Theism and Atheism	2
Beliefs	4
Ethics	5
Consciousness	6
Does Faith have a Future?	9

Chapter 2. The Mystery of Reality	**12**
What is Reality?	12
Changing Perceptions of Reality	12
Reality as Universal Flux	16
Reality and Theories	19
The Mystery of Thought	21
Thought related to Things	23
The Field of Knowledge which has no Physical Referent	28
The Unchanging Element within a Reality that Changes	30
Reality and the Nature of Mind	33
Reality and the Changing Forms in Nature and Thought	38
Fragmentation and Division	41
Reality, Measurement and Values	44

Reality and Creative Intelligence	48
Reality and Being	51
Non-being	56

Chapter 3. Psychological Time — 66

The Nature of Psychological Time and its Relationship to Chronological Time	66
The Nature of Rational and Irrational Thought and Behaviour	69
Psychological time and its Relationship to lack of Conscious Awareness and Genetic Predisposition	74
The Disproportionate Significance given to Psychological Knowledge	77
Psychological Time and its Relationship to Love	79
The Ending of Psychological Time	82

Chapter 4. The Nature of Faith — 87

Faith as Ultimate Concern	87
Idolatrous Faith	87
Ultimate Concern as a Function of Timeless Reality (Beyond Psychological Time)	90
The Nature of the Spiritual and Psychophysical	91
Faith and Reason	95
The Truth of Faith and Scientific Truth	99
The Truth of Faith and Historical Truth	103
The Truth of Faith and Philosophical Truth	105
Faith and Love	109
Faith and Courage	111

Chapter 5. Faith and the Courage to be Oneself — 114

What is a Self?	115

What it means to be Oneself	120
Anxiety	123
The Anxiety of Fate and Death	128
The Anxiety of Emptiness and Meaninglessness	133
The Anxiety of Guilt and Condemnation	136
The Nature of Conscience	137
Guilt and Love	141
Man's Quest for Meaning and an Ultimate Concern	143
Overcoming Despair	145
Love and the Participation in Divine Self-Affirmation	150
Vitality and Courage	152
Courage as a commitment to Love	155

Chapter 6. The Nature of Genuine Religiousness and the Future of Religion — 160

What is Religion?	160
Religion and the Past	162
Religion and Cognitive Limitations	163
Mysticism	166
Mysticism and the Issue of Sin	167
Myth and Metaphor	169
Genuine Religiousness	176
Beyond Theism	181
The Meaning of Prayer in a World with no External Deity	183
The Relationship between Ethics and Religious Faith	185
Genuine Religious Faith and the Future	187

Epilogue. The Having and Being Modes of Living — 194

What is the Having Mode?	194
What is the Being Mode?	195

The Difference between Having and Being	196
Having and Being in the Daily Experience of Life:	197
Learning	197
Conversing	198
Having Knowledge and Knowing	198
Loving	200
The Will to Give, to Share, to Sacrifice	200
Security/Insecurity	204
Sin and Forgiveness	205
Being and the Eternal Now	206
Glossary	209
References	212
Bibliography	217
Index	219

PREFACE

I began to take an interest in spiritual matters in 1971 whilst a chemistry student at Bath University and working on an industrial placement in Johannesburg. One evening, I was listening to the newly-acclaimed production of 'Jesus Christ Superstar' on the radio and this started me thinking about issues connected with religion and the apartheid political system which was adopted in South Africa at that time. When I returned to university in England I started to give more thought to theological issues but found it difficult to make sense of religious dogma which did not coincide with my perceptions of reality. However, I felt a distinct empathy with what Jesus had to say about the way we should live and I admired his character and the courage shown in the way he lived and died.

During my final year at university I worked too hard and this began to take effect on my nervous system. I didn't realise at the time what was happening, becoming very anxious about situations which would not normally have bothered me. I continued to work hard, with an ever-increasing drain on my nervous energy, and as the year progressed I struggled to keep a sense of perspective. The experience, in terms of sheer anxiety, was difficult to deal with as I battled to find the inner strength to hold myself together.

This was the most difficult period of my life but also one

which heralded a new beginning, as it was at that time when I met the girl who was to become my wife. She was a student teacher and helped me to deal with, what seemed at the time, a life-changing ordeal that set me on a spiritual journey. By the time I finished my degree at Bath in 1972 I had come to the realisation that I did not want to pursue a career in industry. I decided to do a Postgraduate Diploma in Education at Sheffield University and, after spending two years as a teacher in secondary education, I transferred into primary education where I ended my career as the Head of a Church School.

Forty years have elapsed since my final year at Bath and ever since then I have been absorbed in a spiritual quest, a search to establish what gives meaning and a sense of purpose to life. During that time I have enjoyed a strong, happy marriage, blessed with two sons, and this has brought me great joy and an insight into the nature and importance of love in the truest sense of the word.

I have also been fortunate enough to read books by certain authors which have struck an inner chord and stimulated my own thinking. It seemed to me that these authors, from various cultural and educational backgrounds, were expressing, in different ways, truths about our perceptions of reality. I sensed a commonality in what they had to say and I decided that, once I retired, I would read these books again, reflect on their content and attempt to define the common ground which they shared.

It was as if what the different authors had to say were like different parts of a musical composition and I wanted to find a way to draw them into harmony. This book is the outcome, in which I have sought to acknowledge and integrate some of their ideas with my own thoughts, in presenting a rational case for religious faith consistent with the mystery of reality. It is not faith as a dogmatic belief, for I will argue that there is no such thing as absolute knowledge. It is faith as the state of ultimate concern, a concept expressed by the theologian Paul Tillich more than fifty years ago.

In recent years a number of authors have written books which have sought to denigrate religion and demonstrate its irrelevance to life in the twenty-first century. One such author is Sam Harris, whose book, "The End of Faith", is highly dismissive of dogmatic theism which he considers to be unethical and a danger to world peace. In Chapter 1, I consider a number of his arguments which are critical of faith in terms of belief systems that bear no relationship to our current perceptions of reality.

He points out, justifiably in my opinion, that most of the problems in this world are linked to our misconception of consciousness as a dualistic process. He believes that our problems would be solved if people could recognise the selflessness of consciousness and bring a rational approach to our deepest personal concerns, which he feels would lead to the end of faith. Whilst I agree entirely that man's problems are rooted in a dualistic interpretation of consciousness, that his spiritual salvation/enlightenment is dependent on a realisation of this misperception, and that there is a need for a rational approach to our deepest personal concerns, I would suggest that this does not herald the end of faith. I shall argue that it is possible to adopt a faith that is rational, empirical and focuses on the dissolution of subject/object duality. This form of faith is not based on dogmatic belief, but on the conception of faith as a state of commitment to what is of ultimate concern. Such a faith is what gives a sense of meaning and direction to life.

Harris would describe himself as an atheist, that is, someone who is opposed to theism. There are, and have been in the past, people within the Church who, like Harris, do not subscribe to theistic beliefs but, nevertheless, have a strong religious faith. In the early years of my own spiritual journey I found that, whilst I could relate to the spiritual insights of Jesus, I could not relate to many of the claims made by the Church on his behalf, which appeared to be framed in a conception of reality which bore no relation to the world in which I was living. Fortunately, I came across a book written by Bishop John Robinson entitled, 'But that I Can't Believe', which reassured me that even Bishops had reservations about what appeared to me to be nonsensical.

More recently, I read 'Why Christianity Must Change or Die', written by the Rev. John Shelby Spong, the former Bishop of Newark in the USA. I related very strongly to what he had to say and to the rational and non-dogmatic manner in which he expressed it. I respected the courage he showed in his challenge of Church doctrines and considered it to be a manifestation of the courage to be oneself. It is interesting to note that both Harris and Spong have great respect for the author and theologian Paul Tillich, but whilst the former is dismissive of faith, the latter has, in my view, a valuable concept of faith. I intend to show why I believe that there is a strong case to support the type of faith to which Spong subscribes.

In order to set the scene, in Chapter 2 I consider the mystery of reality and discuss the thoughts of scientist and philosopher David Bohm. Reality is here considered as a flowing process of which man's perception is both limited and constantly changing. He uses language to express scientific theories, advance religious beliefs or expand on other bodies of knowledge. This gives him the impression that he is able to grasp reality, but the truth of the matter is that it can only be perceived instantly or directly, beyond thought, in the "now" moment. Because the physical receptors that make up our senses have a limited capacity, we fail to take cognizance of a large proportion of the sense data which is accessible to us. In other words, our physical senses are totally inadequate for perceiving reality as it is. It would be a mistake to believe otherwise.

Reality is best described as "a process of undivided wholeness in flowing movement", but man's attempts to describe this phenomenon are distorted by a process of fragmentation, which occurs within consciousness, whereby he perceives himself as an entity, or ego, separate from this flowing process. The lecturer and author J. Krishnamurti called the time we spend in preoccupation with the ego, 'Psychological Time', and in Chapter 3, I discuss this concept and the insidious, toxic effect this can have on the way life is lived.

In Chapter 4, I explore Paul Tillich's view of faith as the state of being ultimately concerned. Consideration is given to how his ideas relate to the process of psychological time and how it is possible to define faith which is consistent with reason and philosophical truth. I also discuss Viktor Frankl's thoughts on unconscious spirituality and how this seeks expression through psychophysical activity, within the world of form in time and space.

In Chapter 5, I continue to explore Tillich's ideas which

relate faith to 'the courage to be', a state of "being" that harnesses a vitality which energizes the individual to personally overcome anxieties and fears. Discussion focuses on what it means to be oneself, how fear and anxiety in their different forms arise through the process of psychological time, and how they are overcome by the manifestation of 'the courage to be' which has its roots in faith as ultimate concern.

In Chapter 6, I consider some of the thoughts of John Hick with regard to the nature of religion and the problem of religions as systems of belief. I explore the concept of genuine religiousness, as a function of the spiritual unconscious, and endeavour to show why this needs to be a personal response to reality as it presents itself in the moment. This is why it is so difficult to express religion in terms of any rigid belief system and why dogmatic fundamentalism is a legacy from the past which bears no relationship to the mystery of reality. Towards the end of this chapter I discuss some of the thoughts of John Shelby Spong which may inspire those who are searching for a spiritual commitment to living.

Faith is pointless unless it is related to the way life is lived and provides a sense of meaning and direction. In 1976 Dr. Erich Fromm, the social philosopher and author wrote an excellent book called "To Have or to Be", which identified two radically different approaches to living. In the Epilogue I discuss the essential features of these modes of living and relate them to the ideas described in previous chapters.

Finally, I wish to clarify my use, in this book, of the generic terms 'man' and 'he' as a general reference for the species Homo sapiens. The use of 'man' in this context is in no way intended to be sexist and implies a sex-undifferentiated reference to the human race. To make constant reference to 'he/she' may, in my opinion, be pedantic, awkward and may irritate the reader.

ACKNOWLEDGEMENTS

Knowledge is a process that is not absolute but evolutionary and builds on what has come before. In the Preface to this book I refer to a number of authors who have been influential in the development of my thoughts and ideas. I should like to express my gratitude to all of them and sincerely hope that I have fully acknowledged and presented their thoughts and ideas in a way which would meet with their approval.

In addition I should like to acknowledge a debt of gratitude to the author Eckhart Tolle. Although I do not refer specifically to his work, I found his books, "The Power of Now" and "A New Earth" extremely helpful in the way they presented the concept of 'ego'. They helped to clarify concepts on Eastern thought, and reinforced the significance of living in the present moment.

Finally, I should like to thank my family, and in particular, my wife Joan and sons, Simon and Jonathan, for the support and encouragement they have given me in this venture. Their love has been a source of insight and inspiration.

HOW TO READ THIS BOOK

Reading this book may present the reader with a number of new concepts. It may well be necessary to read certain passages several times in order to assimilate their content as this is not a book to be read quickly. Some suggestions to anybody reading the book would be as follows:

- Do not read too much at one sitting
- Take time to reflect on what is read in order to assimilate and absorb the concepts
- Read the book several times
- To get the best from the book, discuss the thoughts and ideas with a loved one or within the context of group discussion.

Chapter 2 provides some insight into the thoughts and concepts concerning the mystery of reality that have influenced the development of the ideas featuring later on. As will become apparent, the attempts we make to interpret reality rely much on the use of metaphors and analogies. Where possible, these are used in order to try and give concrete form to abstract ideas about which we have no absolute knowledge. If the reader does find some of the ideas in this chapter a little difficult to come to terms with, then temporarily set them to one side with a view to returning to them later. It may be helpful to return to this chapter retrospectively in order to reflect on how the concepts, described therein, relate to subsequent thinking.

In writing this book I am conscious of how some of my thinking has been influenced by Eastern concepts (such as 'the selflessness of consciousness'). I know from my own experience that these are alien to the Western mind which takes time to get used to them. In view of this, I have deliberately adopted a style of writing which re-visits and attempts to reinforce concepts throughout the book. This must be a legacy of the time I spent as a teacher but reflects a concern to try and get my message over to the reader.

At the end of each chapter, there is a summary of the key ideas which the reader will find useful, and I have included a glossary.

CHAPTER 1.

The End of Faith?

In recent years, a number of books have been published that have dismissed certain religions as antiquated belief systems with no relevance in the twenty-first century. In fact, the authors of these books go as far as to say that, not only are they irrelevant, but are in fact, dangerous. One such author is Sam Harris[1], whose book 'The End of Faith' regards religion as of little more use than alchemy. He argues that most forms of religion lack empirical substance and that, just as alchemy bears no relationship to chemistry, many religious beliefs bear no relationship to other forms of knowledge which have developed and progressed over time.

Harris is scathingly dismissive of the values of the fundamentalist forms of religions such as Judaism, Christianity and Islam, which were founded on, and still subscribe to the world views existing at the times of their inception. He suggests, and I agree, that if religion addresses a genuine sphere of understanding, it should be susceptible to progress and not the mere re-iteration of past doctrine. Furthermore, he believes that religious moderates are dangerous because they do not recognise the need for radical insight, but only wish to dilute ancient superstitions and belief systems that were based on basic ignorance about the world.

It is worth noting that there are, and have been in the past, a number of high profile individuals, within organised religion, who are deeply unhappy with fundamentalist beliefs and the interpretations they place on a faith in God. One such individual is the Rev. John Shelby Spong, who in his book, 'Why Christianity Must Change or Die', describes himself as a Christian in exile. He feels that we can no longer adopt a first century attitude to religion but need to take on board insights of the modern world. He feels that creeds should not be written in stone and need to evolve with man's changing perceptions of reality. He makes an extremely relevant point when he says[2] that any re-casting of the creeds we may produce today will reflect our levels of knowledge and prejudices, and will be no more eternal than those formulations of the fourth and fifth centuries proved to be. Spong, like Harris, suggests that the crux of the problem is our interpretation of the word God, which from early times has been defined in theistic terms.

Theism and Atheism

Spong[3] defines theism as,

"...belief in an external, personal, supernatural, and potentially invasive Being." He says, *"That is the definition of God literally present in the Hebrew scripture. That is, indeed, the definition that has so captured the popular concept of God that no possibility for God seems to exist beyond the scope of theism. Even our language draws that conclusion. For if a person is not a theist, acknowledging the existence of a being called God, then our language suggests that the only alternative is to be an a-theist."*

Theism developed in response to man's evolving self-consciousness and this is why it has such a powerful influence and hold over the definition of God. This makes sense when you consider that, in most situations man's sense of self is his illusory ego, an insecure creation of the mind which, from early times, sought security through the illusory form of a Cosmic ego, or father-figure (theistic God) to which he attributed human qualities. Therefore, the death of theism feels like the death of God.

The development of self-consciousness led to an awareness of mortality and meaninglessness. The perception of these aspects of reality was traumatic and religion developed as a coping mechanism to manage the shock of these realisations. Religious truth was said to have been revealed by God, was infallible and therefore not subject to debate. The theistic definition of God came into existence as a response to human need, but man has evolved to a point where the theistic God concept needs to be replaced by a concept which is more attuned to perceptions of reality in the twenty-first century. The spiritual dimension to life needs to be expressed, or re-framed, in ways which appear 'really real' to our cognitive structures.

Harris believes that the God who is the focal point of the religions developed in the Middle East has been the source of nothing but bloodshed and suffering, and that religious conflict held back the development of civilisation. Various prophets from the past such as Moses, Jesus and Mohammed were perceived as God's messengers who conveyed his wishes to the people. Those who were followers of their specific creed felt that they were special in God's eyes and that, if they were obedient to God's laws, they would be rewarded when the time came for them to leave this world. Faithful followers would move on to a glorious existence in paradise, whereas infidels would be condemned to an eternity of torment in hell. Followers recorded the words of the prophets in the books deemed to be holy and free from error.

Harris[4] says,

"Epistemological black holes of this sort are fast draining the light from our world...The belief that certain books were written by God leaves us powerless to address the most potent source of human conflict, past and present."

The mystery of reality would suggest that nobody possesses absolute truth and the whole mind-set of fundamentalist thinking appears to be based on an authoritarian, anthropocentric, theistic view of God, as a father who disciplines and punishes his children when they are naughty and rewards them when they are good. The Bible says that God created man in his own image and I believe that there might be some truth in this statement, depending on how you interpret the word 'God', but the real problem seems to be that man has created God in his own image. If that sounds paradoxical it is because I believe that man's essential self (a function of "being") is grounded in "Being-itself" (an aspect of reality which we could call God), but man's image of God is a product of his illusory self or ego.

Beliefs

Harris says that to believe in the existence of God is to believe that we stand in some relation to his existence. However, to refer to God in terms of *His* existence presents a semantic problem because it implies a theistic view of God as a noun with a personal nature. This is a subject/object conception of reality whereby man, as a subject, views God, as an object, who is the creator of the world (what we call subject/object duality). If our beliefs are attempts to represent states of the world, they must stand in the right relation to the world to be valid. It seems to me that it is impossible to have any fixed beliefs about God and we shall return to this subject later when we discuss the nature of faith as ultimate concern.

Harris[5] attacks the theistic concept of God as portrayed in scripture and is critical of the claims made on his behalf. I agree with him that the problem of vindicating an almighty and all-knowing God in the face of evil is insurmountable and that man's attempts to rationalise the problem lack credibility.

Ethics

Harris[6] suggests that a rational approach to ethics becomes possible once we realise that questions of right and wrong are really questions about the happiness and suffering of sentient beings. If we are able to affect the happiness or suffering of others, we have ethical responsibilities toward them. He believes that the idea that religion is somehow the source of our deepest ethical intuitions is absurd, but I will argue that faith, based on ultimate concern, has love and compassion as its foundation and that anybody who builds their life on that foundation is essentially religious, whether they realise it or not.

Consciousness

Harris is not dismissive of a spiritual dimension to life, only of the way in which this is conceived in the form of a theistic God who lords it over the universe. He rejects this interpretation of reality and I find myself agreeing with much of what he has to say. However, whereas he feels that the realisation of the selflessness of consciousness leads to the end of faith, I believe that it is the foundation on which faith is built. What do we mean by the selflessness of consciousness and what do we mean when we talk about a "self"? These are important questions which we shall seek to explore more fully in due course.

Consciousness is the condition in which thought, emotion and our sense of self arises and we are aware of sights, sounds, sensations, feelings, moods and thoughts. Harris suggests that if we can learn to recognise our identity as consciousness itself, and not the thoughts and emotions, if we are able to stand back and observe these appearances, instead of getting caught up in them, we shall be able to rise above the changing fortunes of fate and everyday existence. However, we have an abiding sense of self which we call 'I' which inhabits a body and perceives itself to be separate from experience. Every act of perception or cognition appears to be the activity of a subject that knows, but is separate from what is known. This subject (the thinker of thoughts or the knower of what is known) relates to everything within the terms of a subject/object relationship, whether the object is part of its body (my leg), a possession (my house), an experience (my memories) or even God. Whatever the relationship actually is between consciousness and the body, it is clear that something is happening to distort the apprehension of this reality.

This sounds complicated, so let us see if we can develop a clearer picture.

Diagram (a)
Subject/Object Duality
Sense of Self

Diagram (b)
Loss of Subject/Object Perception
Loss of a sense of Self

Person 'X'
- Thoughts known by the 'knower'
- Subject 'I' illusory self or ego
- Object 'Me'

Person 'Y'
- Consciousness. Experience. Present moment awareness
- Loss of subject/object perception
- Self is the activity of 'being', the current experience. There is no 'experiencer' of the experience because such an entity does not exist
- Brain not cognizant of a sense of 'me' and completely involved with current experience or productive thought.

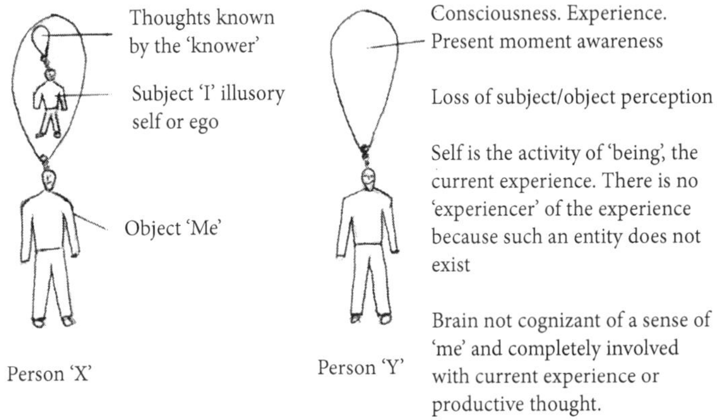

Figure 1.1

In Figure 1.1, (a) represents the mode of existence that nearly all of us adopt for most of our waking time. Person 'X' has a mental image of whom he perceives himself to be, the person he perceives to inhabit his physical form, which provides him with a self-concept that he calls 'I'. When he is thinking about something, he believes that it is this illusory image which he calls 'I', who is doing the thinking and this gives rise to the perception of subject/object duality. This sense of 'self' seems to be the product of the brain's representing its own acts of representation; its seeing of the world generates an image of a one who sees, a knower behind the known.

According to neuroscience there is no region in the brain which acts as a master controller who is directing proceedings.

However, it is possible to form a representation of the world without the individual forming a representation of himself in the world (see Person 'Y' in (b)). Loss of self is characterised by a loss of subject/object perception and although the flow of experience continues, the sense of an "I" experiencing the experience is missing.

If you look at it carefully, you will see that consciousness, the thing you call 'I', is really a stream of experiences, of sensations, thoughts, dispositions, traits and feelings in constant motion (we shall return to this subject later). These experiences, which include memories, can impinge upon consciousness in a reflective way and give the impression that 'I' is something of substance. This eventually leads to the sense of an entity, a self that knows. This phantom self, the knower, can often be threatened or disturbed by what it knows. If we try and search for this self that knows, what we call "I", we discover that it does not exist, it is an illusion. The philosopher Hume said,

"When I enter most intimately into what I call myself...I can never catch myself at any time without a perception."

It seems to me that Hume is expressing a fundamental truth, which neuroscience appears to confirm, that the self is not an object or a thing that can be observed. He was looking for the experiencer of the experience but all he could find was the activity of experience which suggests that he can only perceive himself through some form of activity. Alan Watts implies that we are what we experience, for example, when we feel angry we are anger at that point in time. When we feel joyful we are joy. The moment we try to analyse the experience, to find the experiencer of the experience, we cannot find it and the experience has passed.

Harris[7] suggests, and I agree, that most people live in a state where they experience this duality of subject and object most of their lives, and the world consists of billions of people, each with a personal sense of "I" and competing points of view. This feeling of separateness and insecurity encourages like-minded individuals to form groups, based on religious, national or other interests, with their associated collective egos and rigid boundaries. Ego identification leads to conflict and it is difficult to see how this will end, especially while groups hang onto the beliefs of the past which give them a strong sense of identity. It will need a mass change in consciousness for people to realise that we are part of the process or flux of life, inextricably linked to each other.

Clearly the way forward is liberation from the illusion of the self as a separate entity, something that the East has been aware of for thousands of years through the teachings of the Buddha and other great philosopher mystics. The fundamental insight of Eastern wisdom is the understanding that failure to continually recognise thoughts as thoughts, moment after moment, is what gives each of us the feeling that we call "I" and is the source of unhappiness and suffering.

Does Faith have a Future?

Harris[8] believes that once we recognise the selflessness of consciousness it should be possible to bring reason, spirituality and ethics together in our thinking about the world. I agree that this would be the beginning of a rational approach to our deepest personal concerns, but whereas Harris believes that this will lead to the end of faith, I believe that this is a foundation on which faith can be built. It is significant to note that Harris[9] makes it clear that he is criticising faith in its ordinary, scriptural sense-as belief in, and life orientation toward certain historical and metaphysical propositions. He emphasises that he has no quarrel with the approach to faith advocated by the theologian Paul Tillich, or with anybody who seeks to define it in a way which brings it into conformity with some rational ideal.

Harris deprecates the lack of empiricism in religious belief and castigates certain forms of behaviour which are advocated in its name. Many people will relate to, and agree with much of what he says and will feel that there is no place for religious faith in the modern world. However, Harris himself alludes to the fact that his argument is aimed at the majority of the faithful in every religious tradition, not at what he calls '*Tillich's blameless parish of one.*' Here, I suspect that he would find some common ground with John Shelby Spong whose approach to faith rests on the foundations laid by Paul Tillich.

When Harris talks about a rational approach to our deepest personal concerns leading to the end of faith, he is referring to faith as dogmatic belief, in the scriptural sense. Tillich did not equate faith with belief and defined it as that which is of ultimate concern. It is my intention to show that, in spite of our limited ability to perceive reality as it is, and the limitations of language, it is still possible to define religious faith as a process that is rational, ethical and gives a sense of direction and meaning to the way we live.

Summary of Key Ideas

- Theism presents a view of God as a personal, supernatural and a potentially controlling Being.
- The theistic concept of God is a product of subject/object duality, a view of reality where an individual subject, 'I', views God as an 'object' or entity/Being who has a separate existence to himself.
- There is another way of viewing reality, called selfless consciousness, whereby the perception of a sense of self is missing. The individual is conscious of sense perceptions, and experiences reality but not from the perspective of a separate 'I'. He flows with the experiences of life but not from the perspective of an ego.
- When we understand the implications of the selflessness of consciousness this raises problems with a theistic conception of God.
- The author Sam Harris believes that once we recognise the selflessness of consciousness this will lead to the end of faith, whereas I propose to show that this is a foundation on which faith can be built.

CHAPTER 2.

The Mystery of Reality

What is Reality?

If you were to ask the ordinary man in the street the question, "What is reality?" I suspect that you would get some quizzical looks. It is not something that many of us consider, and if we do, we probably do not spend too much time pondering an answer to what is a very deep question. Most people would probably suggest that reality is 'what is', that which is happening around them, a process in which they participate. This would appear to be reasonable and would imply that they knew, or were able to perceive exactly what is happening, but reality appears to be different things to different people. Why do we all have different perceptions and viewpoints? Is it possible to know reality as it really is, and what implications does this have for the way we live and the beliefs or faith which we may, or may not hold? These are some of the questions which this book has set out to explore.

Changing Perceptions of Reality

Our perception of reality is strongly influenced by the culture in which we live and by the world-views which it promotes. If we are not careful we tend to assume that we interpret reality as it really is and we are unaware of how our limited senses and brain filter out, or fail to perceive vast amounts of sense data. We are often unaware of how our perceptions are shaped by the unconscious assumptions that we make which are related to the paradigms which comprise our conceptual frameworks. A paradigm is another word for a theory, or frame of reference that gives meaning to our perceptions and can influence the perceptions we make within our environment.

Stephen Covey[1] gives a good illustration of how our perceptions are influenced by past experience. He took a group of people and divided them into two groups. He showed one group the image of a beautiful woman and the other the image of an old hag. He then presented them with a composite image (Figure 2.1), which contained the two images, and asked them to describe what they could see. It was significant that their answer was related to the image that they had first seen (i.e. those who had initially seen the beautiful woman perceived her image in the composite image and vice-versa).

Figure 2.1

During the course of history man has observed and tried to make sense of his environment. The development of language has enabled him to express his perceptions in terms of thought, concepts and theories which, in turn, have facilitated communication with his fellow man. However, he believes that his use of language is able to define reality, that the cognitive structures and paradigms that influence his behaviour are stable and true, until something happens to make him question their validity.

This has been the pattern which has defined the development of most forms of knowledge, especially science, and at different points in history, various key figures have appeared on the scene whose genius has transformed the way we look at reality. For example, it was generally accepted that the Earth was at the centre of the universe until Copernicus, through careful observation of the stars and planets, discovered that this was not true. Our perception of the world of science has changed radically during the past three hundred years and will undergo further changes in the future.

Indeed, Lynn Mc Taggart says that we are on the brink of another scientific revolution which is every bit as profound as Einstein's theory of relativity. She says[2],

"Human beings and all living things are a coalescence of energy in a field of energy connected to every other thing in the world. This pulsating energy field is the central engine of our being and our consciousness, the alpha and the omega of our existence.

There is no 'me' and 'not me' duality to our bodies in relation to the universe, but one underlying energy field. This field is responsible for our mind's highest functions, the

information source guiding the growth of our bodies".

McTaggart points out that, up until recently, much of scientific thinking was influenced by ideas that were formulated in the seventeenth century, a world view of separateness where matter was divided into particles and separate from the mind. Similarly, God was perceived as a separate entity that existed around his creation. Our body, like the universe, was perceived as a well-oiled machine and separate from our consciousness with a mind able to stand outside "reality" and observe it objectively. The view of biology and medicine, which up until now has been dominated by Newtonian and Cartesian thought, is under review. We are developing a view of the world which is able to explain observed phenomena (e.g. synchronicity) which were incomprehensible in terms of the old paradigms.

In recent years, a number of scientists experimenting in different fields have sought a common explanation to their findings in terms of what has been called the Zero Point Field. This perceives the universe as one sea of energy in which everything is connected to everything else. At a fundamental level, living beings, including humans, are packets of quantum energy interacting with and exchanging energy with the sea of energy that surrounds them. McTaggart says that it would appear that cellular communication, even our minds operate according to quantum processes and that perception occurs as a result of interactions between the subatomic particles in our brains with the quantum sea of energy, in a form of resonance. However, the concept of energy is itself a mystery that is defined rather vaguely as a capacity for activity which manifests itself in different forms.

What the new paradigm in science is saying is that, at a fundamental level, each of us is connected with each other and the world at the level of our "being". The world, at its most basic, exists as a complex web of interdependent relationships which are indivisible. This is a difficult concept to understand because our senses play a significant role in the way we perceive reality and we are generally unconscious of their limitations.

Reality as Universal Flux

One of the foremost scientific thinkers and philosophers of our time was David Bohm and according to him, reality should not be conceived of as a 'thing' but should be understood as a process. He says[3]

"Not only is everything changing, but all is flux. That is to say, 'what is' is the process of becoming itself, while all objects, events, entities, conditions, structures, etc., are forms that can be abstracted from this process."

He[4] implies that reality is a flowing process of universal flux or energy which leads to the creation of matter, nature and thought which is not static but in a state of constant change. This is a view which brings to mind the Taoist conception of Tao which is likened to a great flowing stream. Bohm, a nuclear physicist, says that new developments in physics imply the need to look at the world as an undivided whole and that the old atomistic form of insight is a simplification and an abstraction, valid only in a limited context.

Referring to the 'stream of consciousness', a flux of awareness which is not precisely definable, he draws attention to the definable forms of thoughts and ideas that form and dissolve in this flux like ripples, waves and vortices in a flowing stream. Some thoughts recur and persist in a stable way while others are transient or evanescent. Bohm is proposing that this analogy expresses a general form of insight which is applicable to matter.

If you have stood alongside a flowing river you will probably have noticed the different forms that appear in the water as ripples, waves and whirlpools. Each ripple or whirlpool has a form that is visible and makes it appear to be a separate entity but each is, in essence, a shape or form that is composed of water that is part of the flowing river. Some forms, such as whirlpools, can appear to be more permanent than other forms, like ripples, which suddenly appear and then disappear. Bohm suggests that there is a universal flux that cannot be defined explicitly but which gives form to explicit shapes, some stable and some unstable which can be abstracted from this flux.

We are conscious of the fact that matter takes up different forms, some stable like rock and others unstable like gunpowder. Matter interacts with energy, both physically and chemically, and changes its form, so it is clear that there is a relationship between matter and energy. Only small amounts of energy, in the form of electrical discharges, are required to change the chemical form of substances like dynamite, whereas large amounts of heat energy are required to change the physical form of rock and turn it into magma. In a situation involving extreme energy change, such as in an atomic explosion, solid material can change state to become invisible to the eye.

Bohm's concept of energy giving rise to different forms

is consistent with what we observe empirically. However, it is extremely difficult for us to visualise our existence in terms of the manifestation of different forms of energy which animate and give form to our physical body. The reason why different forms in nature adopt specific structures which are energy-related, and how they manifest this form within a universal sea of energy is a complete mystery which is difficult to comprehend.

According to Bohm, mind and matter are not separate substances but different aspects of one whole and unbroken movement of energy. However, in spite of the undivided wholeness in flowing movement, the various patterns which can be seen within it have a certain relative autonomy and stability in terms of thought and matter. Hence, he says that, in specified contexts, we can adopt various forms of insight to allow simplification of certain things, and to treat them momentarily and for certain limited purposes, as if they were autonomous and stable, as well as perhaps separately existent. He suggests that we must be careful not to fall into the trap of looking at ourselves and the whole world in this way which leads to the illusion that reality is of a fragmentary nature.

I believe that part of the reason why man creates illusions about reality is related to his limited powers of perception. For example, his eyes are a great asset and help him to function within the context of everyday living but they are limited in their capacity to perceive reality. Until recently, the existence of germs was unknown and it was only the development of the microscope which enabled man to discover their existence. Science, in its early days, conceived matter to be comprised of solid building blocks called atoms.

We now know that this is not the case and that the matter from which our physical body is formed has little solid content. According to modern physics it appears to be comprised of packets of energy which interact in some mysterious way, and are perceived by the senses to take the form of a solid organism that is separate from other organisms and materials within the environment. If eyes were sufficiently sensitive they would perceive the body to be a whirling mass of energy. The lack of sensitivity, which fails to perceive the presence of germs, is totally unable to perceive reality at a sub-atomic level.

Bohm's conception of a flowing universal flux or field of energy, in which different configurations or bundles of energy attain separate forms within the context of the whole and later dissolve, or disperse in the flowing stream of the flux, is a powerful metaphor which is consistent with the scientific revolution alluded to by McTaggart.

Reality and Theories

Bohm makes reference to what he calls 'fragmentary thinking' which reflects man's limited ability to think in a clear unambiguous way. This is brought about by his universal habit of mistaking the content of his thought to be 'a description of the world as it is'. We have just illustrated the limitations of man's sensual, discriminatory powers with regard to sight but, in spite of this, he still believes that there is a direct correlation between the content of his thought and objective reality. The relationship between thought and reality is tenuous and far from straightforward.

Any theory (scientific or otherwise) is primarily a form

of insight and not a form of knowledge of how the world is. Scientific theories come and go and last as long as they are capable of providing an explanation for man's worldly observations. When they no longer coincide with his perception of reality they have to be modified or replaced by alternative paradigms which provide a better explanation of observed phenomena. Newtonian theory provided a form of insight which worked well for several centuries and still does for observations on a macroscopic scale. However, it was found to be inadequate for explaining phenomena at a sub-atomic level where relativity and quantum theory were insights that provided a better explanation.

Bohm emphasises that one cannot say Newtonian theory was the truth up to around 1900, after which it suddenly became false, while relativity and quantum theory suddenly became the truth. Theories are insights which are neither true nor false. Man is continually developing new forms of insight which are clear up to a point in certain contexts but which can lose their usefulness when applied to other different domains. Theories should be viewed as ways of looking at the world (i.e. world-views), rather than as 'absolutely true knowledge of how things are'.

Bohm[5] says that the factual information that we obtain from the world will be shaped by the theories which influence our observations, or, putting it another way, our theoretical insights provide the main source of organisation of our factual knowledge (e.g. light can be perceived as particle or wave-form depending on experimental expectation). We must maintain an awareness of how our experience is shaped by the insight provided by the theories that are implicit or explicit in our general ways of thinking. For example, if we perceive from past experience that someone is devious and of questionable character, we are likely to be suspicious of their behaviour, especially if they appear to be helpful. We may suspect that they have ulterior motives when, in reality, their intentions may be genuine. Our perception of the reality of a given situation may well be distorted by inappropriate pre-conceptions.

The Mystery of Thought

Bohm[6] makes the point that knowledge is an abstraction from the one total flux which is the ground both of reality and the knowledge of this reality. All knowledge is produced, communicated and applied in thought but what is the process of thought?

It would seem that thought is basically a material process and inseparable from electrical and chemical activity in the brain and nervous system. It appears to be related to interaction between the brain, perception and the conceptual frameworks within the mind to which it has access. This evokes memory which includes the intellectual, emotional, muscular and physical responses to memory. All these contribute towards a response of memory to each actual situation which, in turn, fosters further contributions to memory which influence subsequent thinking. Thought considered in this way is basically mechanical, being either a repetition of some existent conceptual structure or fact, or else the arrangement or organisation of these memories into further conceptual structures or ideas.

The perception of whether any thought is relevant requires the operation of a form of energy which we call intelligence. This energy is able to perceive, or create a new structure which is not just a modification of what is already known or present in the memory. It is responsible for the 'Eureka moment' when, after a period of trying to solve a baffling problem, a solution suddenly appears in a flash of inspiration which reveals the irrelevance of previous thinking. This insight, which is essentially an act of perception rather than thought process (though later it can be expressed in thought), leads to the development of a different approach in which all the elements seem to fit a new conceptual structure or paradigm.

Bohm[7] suggests that when thought functions on its own it is mechanical and not intelligent because it imposes its own generally irrelevant order drawn from memory. Thought, however, is capable of responding, not only from memory but also to the unconditioned perception of intelligence. Bohm believes that if intelligence is to be an unconditioned act of perception, its ground cannot be in structures such as cells, molecules, atoms etc. He suggests that the ground of intelligence must be in the undetermined and unknown flux that is also the ground of all definable forms of matter.

In order to make his point, Bohm[8] draws a convincing analogy with a radio receiver. He says,

"When the output of the receiver 'feeds back' into the input, the receiver operates on its own, to produce mainly irrelevant and meaningless noise, but when it is sensitive to the signal on the radio wave, its own order of inner movement of electric currents (transformed into sound waves) is parallel to the order in the signal and thus the receiver serves to bring a meaningful order originating beyond the level of its own

structure into movements on the level of its own structure. One might then suggest that in intelligent perception, the brain and nervous system respond directly to an order in the universal and unknown flux that cannot be reduced to anything that could be defined in terms of knowable structures."

He believes that intelligence and material process have a single origin, which is the unknown totality of the universal flux. He implies that what have been commonly called mind and matter are abstractions from the universal flux, and that both are to be regarded as different and relatively autonomous orders within the one whole movement. He asserts that it is thought responding to intelligent perception which is capable of bringing about an overall harmony or fitting between mind and matter.

Thought related to Things

If thought is a material process which may be more relevant when it operates in conjunction with intelligence, then what is the relationship between thought and reality? It is a common belief that there is a reflective correspondence of thought with 'real things' which creates a copy or image of these things. Eastern wisdom has recognised the illusory nature of such a belief, and Bohm[9] adopts a similar viewpoint.

He believes that if the thing and the thought about it have their ground in the one indefinable and unknown totality of flux, then any attempt to explain their relationship by supposing that the thought is in reflective correspondence with the thing has no meaning, because both thought and thing are forms abstracted from the total process. He suggests that the reason why these forms are related could only be in the ground from which they arise. However, there can be no way of discussing reflective correspondence in this ground, because reflective correspondence implies knowledge, while the ground is beyond what can be assimilated in the content of knowledge.

If this is the case, what is the relationship between thought and thing? If thought and matter are forms which are abstracted from the universal flux their essence must be energy. Matter, as a specific form of energy, interacts with other energy forms (e.g. light, sound and heat) and responds in ways that emit energy, or manifest physical or chemical changes which are perceived by our physical senses (e.g. we can see that ice melts or paper burns). These energy signals are processed by our nervous system and brain, interact with the configurations of energy which form the conceptual structures in the mind, and manifest as human thought.

This is clearly an indefinite process dependent on the range of signals for which the individual has appropriate receptors, and also on the mind's range of conceptual energy configurations which can respond to these signals. Where there is a miss-match between perceptual signals and the conceptual energy configurations stored in the mind, this leads to a lack of understanding and the process becomes analogous to fitting square pegs in round holes. Initially, the brain may try to match perceptions to available conceptual patterns but fail to find a link (a bit like trying to match a piece of a jigsaw puzzle that does not fit). Intelligent perception may well interact with the mind, in some way (through the brain), to change the energy configuration of a conceptual framework, or create a new one which facilitates linkage with the new perception.

It is a bit like creating, or finding a jigsaw puzzle to which the new perceptual piece can be matched. This does not mean that there will be no need to create further 'jigsaw puzzles' in the future. To the contrary, man's existence is a continuing story of creating different puzzles or pictures to match his changing perceptions and this leads to the evolution of his conceptions of reality. The above analogy is extremely simplistic as reality will be related to a complex interaction of energy forms.

In considering the relationship between thought and thing, Bohm[10] draws an analogy with the dance of the bees in which one bee is able to indicate the location of honey-bearing flowers to other bees. He suggests that this dance is an activity which does not convey direct knowledge to the 'minds' of the bees, in terms of a reflective correspondence with the flowers, but acts as a pointer or indicator, disposing the bees to an order of action that will eventually lead to the production of honey. He proposes that thought could be viewed as a sort of 'dance of the mind' which functions indicatively, and which, when properly carried out, leads to harmony and order in the process of life. He says that in practical affairs, this harmony and order will result in a community which will be successful in producing food, clothing, shelter, healthy conditions of life, etc.

If we accept Bohm's idea that reality is grounded in a universal flux of energy from which thought and matter are abstractions, what implications may this have for the way man interprets reality? Man interacts with his environment, receiving sense perceptions in the form of energy, which his brain, in conjunction with his mind and intelligent perception, processes and organises into concepts and knowledge. He uses this knowledge to interact with and change his environment and this leads to new perceptions which, under the influence of intelligent perception, change his conceptions of reality.

It would appear that the energy of his thought interacts with the energy of his environment to create a dance of the mind that creates ever-changing energy forms (in terms of conceptual energy configurations) which provide him with knowledge that evolves. This is a process which changes with time and influences his behaviour, whether this concerns his relationships with other human beings or the way he interacts with the material world. The above suggests that man's thinking is integrally linked to the environment, in a way which is caught up in an intricate relationship between different forms of energy.

Here we appear to be talking primarily about a relationship between thought and matter concerning things that have a physical referent or stimulate the physical senses. The universal flux is creative and gives form to matter and thought, or what has been called 'the manifest', whilst maintaining a potential for creative activity which is unmanifest. Man is able to observe the properties of matter and develop concepts which enable him to use it in a creative and practical way. He is also able to interact socially with his fellow human beings and develop conventions, based on thoughts and concepts, which influence his behaviour. By utilising the properties of different materials and adopting appropriate forms of personal and social organisation, he is able to manufacture a wide range of products to meet his needs in terms of food, clothing, housing, medicines etc., and to organise and change his environment.

It would appear that the relationship between man's

thinking and material reality is an interactive process involving energy, but what about thought that arises beyond an interaction between his senses and the physical environment? What about thought that could be considered to be imaginary and unrelated to perceptions made through the physical senses? There is a need to try and draw a distinction between what is real or illusory.

Bohm[11] makes reference to the difficulty a young child can have in drawing a distinction between the content of his thought of what is real and what is imaginary. It takes time for some children to establish the difference between thoughts that relate to situations that are 'real' (i.e. thoughts about something) and those which are imaginary and have no substance. He suggests that the evolution of thought from the time of primitive man has undergone a similar process and one might argue that this process is on-going.

As man developed his technical thought in relation to his dealing with things (e.g. his development of tools and weapons), he felt a need to develop his thought about the totality of his experience of life. Thought about the powers of nature and a developing spiritual awareness led him to engage in a kind of thought process without any clear physical referent. This seemed so intense and realistic that he could no longer maintain a clear distinction between what was real or imaginary.

Such experiences led to a sense of confusion which made a rational approach to living difficult and he felt a need to create a clearer picture of his identity, in relation to nature and the transcendent forces which he sensed but could not see. He still has this problem today with regard to what we call the spiritual dimension and ethics and struggles to differentiate between what gives meaning to his existence and what is illusory.

If thought and matter are inter-related forms of energy grounded in the universal flux, what implications does this have for any form of knowledge? Bohm[12] believes that thought with totality as its content will have *"to be considered as an art form, like poetry, whose function is primarily to give rise to a new perception, rather than to communicate reflective knowledge of 'how everything is'. This implies that there can be no more an ultimate form of such thought than there could be an ultimate poem (that would make all further poems unnecessary)."* Knowledge has to be seen as a process with ever-changing form and content.

The Field of Knowledge which has no Physical Referent

The physical sciences develop models and theories based on observations with a physical component which gives rise to sense perceptions (e.g. matter such as ice will be seen to melt or change form when heated). What do we do in the case of a subject like religion that concerns what we call the spiritual dimension and has no physical referent? Here we are talking about unmanifest reality, something unknown and of uncertain existence. We are unable to utilise the five senses to locate this phenomenon so how will we be able to make our perceptions? And assuming that these could be made, how will we be able to express them conceptually in thoughts and organise these into a coherent body of knowledge? Furthermore, what methods will we use to test the authenticity of this knowledge and determine whether it is real or imaginary?

Knowledge is a product of mind activity that, when it remains open to intelligent perception, undergoes a process of evolution or change that leads to ever more sophisticated theories about the nature of the universe. The study of a subject like religion precludes the use of the five senses, but we would appear to have, what is described as, an intuitive 'sixth sense' which acts as a conduit between the world of form and unmanifest reality. I believe that we can learn to develop this faculty in order to cultivate an awareness of the universal flux.

It is interesting to note that Harris[13] discusses the validity of intuition and believes that we cannot do without it. He says that the traditional opposition between reason and intuition is a false one, that reason is itself intuitive, as any judgement that a proposition is "reasonable" or "logical" relies on intuition to find its feet. Scientists and philosophers talk about *a priori* facts that are fundamental assumptions about the nature of reality which are assumed intuitively. I believe that intuition, as a function of intelligent perception, is an unconscious process which facilitates communication between the timeless dimension of unmanifest reality and manifested form. Quantum energy, from the universal flux, is mysteriously translated into a manifested form of insight which the brain strives to integrate into our cognitive structures, in order to create meaning.

If intuition is a valid process which can lead to connectivity and a sense of unity with reality, why is there so much division and disharmony in the world? The answer lies in the fact that the vast majority of the human race fail to recognise, or choose to ignore the concept of intuition and are unable to utilise this function for reasons which will become clear when we discuss the nature of psychological time.

Part of the problem is rooted in what Bohm[14] has called fragmented thinking, where groups of people have frozen their form of thought, fixed their view of reality and left no room for their thought forms to evolve. What Bohm is saying can apply to all forms of thought, scientific or religious. Scientists can adopt a mindset which dominates their thought processes and makes them blind to new insights. The same can be said of different religious groups who believe that they are in sole possession of the truth about reality (God).

If we are to move forward and make progress we must first recognise that reality is not a fixed entity but a flowing process which is beyond absolute knowledge. Although it is in the unknown, all forms of creation are embedded in this reality and experience a connection, analogous to the umbilical cord connecting mother and baby. I believe that in the case of human beings, this 'umbilical cord' is related to what is often referred to as the soul that links our manifested form with the unmanifested dimension of reality.

The Unchanging Element within a Reality that Changes

When we observe nature we see cyclical patterns which accompany the change in seasons and the processes of birth and death. We observe a moving process in which pattern is accompanied by change, in what appears to be a dynamic situation that leads to an evolution of form in terms of matter (nature) and thought. This is indicative of the fact that reality is a flowing, creative process that cannot be fixed in terms of thought forms which find their origin in this moving flux. Any descriptions of reality will need to take the form of artistic impressions which include models (e.g. scientific models). However, if this is the case, how does this affect our perception of values? Are we to assume that they are transient, subject to evolution, and is it the case that there are no such things as absolute values? When we consider the metaphor of reality as a flowing stream or river, is there any element in the metaphor which has a constant, unchanging quality? I believe that there is.

The content of a stream or river is essentially water which finds its way into the river through rainfall and reaches its destination when it flows back into the sea or ocean. This cycle is a process that continues indefinitely unless affected by climate change. Every form that can be perceived in the flowing river is a function of different variables which include the rate of flow of the current, the nature of obstacles in the river and the physical properties of water itself. We know, for example, that water (at atmospheric pressure) freezes at 0 degrees C., boils at 100 degrees C., has a density of 1g./cm3, has a certain viscosity and displays surface tensional effects. These are fairly constant and will play a part in determining the forms that are possible. Each form that is created in the river is inextricably linked to the unchanging properties of the water but will also depend on the physical layout of the river and rates of flow of the water. Could it be that certain properties of the universal flux are constant (like the physical properties of water) and unchanging within this flowing process which we call reality? Could it also be the case that human forms of creation are conscious of an unchanging element that underlies and gives life to their form, something which can remain hidden, masked by the sensual illusion of individuality but nevertheless, an integral part of all forms of life? Could it be that this unchanging element is the essence of our "being", something we share with all living creatures?

It is my conviction that "being" (the energy which gives life to our form), is grounded in an infinite source that Tillich calls 'Being-itself' (is this the reality to which we refer when we use the word 'God'?), that is a timeless, unchanging element within a universal flux which manifests change. It is the awareness of our essence as "being", that is grounded in the infinite essence of "Being-itself" within the universal flux, that draws us to seek a relationship with that which created and sustains our form.

Furthermore, I believe that it is through intuition that we recognise that there is a link between our spirit, or life energy and the universal flux (or "Ground of Being" or "Being-itself") and that we share this reality with all of humanity. It is when we recognise, and truly acknowledge, that this life energy is the common denominator which we share with mankind and the universal flux that we begin to gain some insight into the true meaning of the word 'love'.

Love is a form of synchronous resonance or bonding between the life energy or spirit (spiritual energy/"being") of the individual with that of other individuals and the "Ground of Being". It is a sense of relatedness to a shared participation in the process of "being", or the acknowledgement of a shared essence. Love is a function of "being", an unchanging spiritual property of the universe (like the physical property of gravitation), that draws us into a relationship, at the level of our "being", toward each other and the "Ground of Being". The truth of this phenomenon, although it can be grasped intellectually, is not experienced primarily through the mind but ontologically in the depths of our "being", at soul level, and is perceived as a feeling of joy and peace, located in the vicinity of the heart. The purpose of life is related to living in a way in which the changing activity of our form, in time and space, is resonant with the unchanging spiritual reality of love.

Reality and the Nature of Mind

It should be clear that there is no reflective correspondence between thought and things, or thought and reality, and that the limitations of our powers of perception make it impossible to know reality as it is. Bohm has suggested that thought, in the form of language, produces a fuzzy picture, a form of knowledge that, although it is not absolute, can act as an indicator that, if used wisely, can enable man to interact intelligently with his environment.

Bohm refers to thought as 'a dance of the mind' but what do we really know about the mind and how it functions? Deepak Chopra[15] says,

"Everything that we experience as material reality is born in an invisible realm beyond space and time, a realm revealed by science to consist of energy and information. This invisible source of all that exists is not an empty void but the womb of creation itself. Something creates and organises this energy. It turns the chaos of quantum soup into stars, galaxies, rain forests, human beings, and our own thoughts, emotions, memories and desires."

Chopra says that even though we can identify the memory centres of the brain, no one has ever proved that memory is stored there. He says[16] that Canadian brain surgeon, Wilder Penfield came to the conclusion that the mind must be a kind of energy field that includes the brain and perhaps even controls it. As there is, no doubt, some link between energy and information, Chopra believes that in place of energy field, we should say "information field," because the brain processes information that is flowing and related to all that exists. When we talk about fields (such as magnetic fields) it brings to mind invisible forms of energy which flow out into space in a state of flux. This is consistent with Bohm's concept of the universal flux and with much of the current scientific thinking discussed by Lynn McTaggart.

In view of the above is it possible to develop a feasible working model of the nature of mind and how it might function? *The first thing we will need to recognise is that our thinking will be metaphorical, an art form and not a precise description of 'reality as it is'.* We are seeking to create a picture which attempts to make sense of our perceptions of reality and offers a way of explaining what we experience in day to day living.

Man is aware that he is in possession of a facility which is a 'receptacle' for his thoughts and ideas and it has generally been assumed that this is located within the brain itself. But is this actually the case? We know that energy is capable of generating magnetic fields whose effects can be measured but not seen, and we also know that information can be stored magnetically. In view of this, is it not conceivable that the energy of our "being" could be capable of generating invisible energy fields within or surrounding the physical matter that comprises our body? Could it not be that each of us has a particular mind which is a form of energy field, capable of storing information and that this is linked, in some way, to the physical brain which acts to process the information stored within it? It seems to me quite feasible that information or memory could be a form of immaterial energy, stored within an energy field, which could be drawn into consciousness through the agency of a material brain.

Intelligent perception (acting independently or through brain activity) could act on this information and change its structure, leading to modified conceptual frameworks or patterns of energy which could then be stored in the mind field. After all, matter itself is energy, and although the brain appears to have a solid or liquid composition, it is in reality a hive of energetic activity. The whole process must be so complex that it is highly unlikely that we shall ever be able to form a true picture of the reality of the situation. The best we can hope for is to create ever more sophisticated models to improve our explanation of our perceptions of reality.

The process of mind appears to have something in common with the memory of a lap-top computer. A person working on a 'lap-top' generates thoughts which are typed into the computer, stored in its memory and forgotten until they decide to reactivate them by returning to the computer. They review the thoughts, modify or even change them completely, storing any changes in the computer memory. The computer is carried around with them and the information that is stored within it remains available should they wish to access it at any time. They might not choose to make use of it for a long time and it may remain dormant, but it is still stored and ready to be re-activated. The analogy breaks down, to some degree, in so far as our real memory tends to be imprecise and subject to distortion and corruption by the brain. However, is it conceivable that the mind could be likened to a portable computer memory, in so far as it is carried around, but is not a material part of the person?

We have suggested that the universal flux is a source of energy whose effects extend throughout the universe. Could it be that such an energy source gives rise to an intelligent energy/information field which gives order to creativity and which could be conceived of as a universal mind? Could it also not be the case that man's particular mind is able to interact with this universal mind? Such a process would be most likely to occur when a sense of unity or resonance exists between man and the "Ground of being" and there is a synchronicity between the energy forms. If we return to our analogy with the lap-top, does this not have something in common with linking to the worldwide web through internet connection? Here again, the analogy has its limitations because any interaction and energy transfer would lack the precision of computer networks.

Chopra[17] believes that we live in a field of awareness which is the potential for life and intelligence. Could it be conceivable that each individual has a localised mind field which is personal to him or her, that these individual fields are capable of interaction with each other and also with a universal mind field of far-reaching proportions? If this were the case, it would explain how individuals think similar thoughts simultaneously and how Newton and Leibnitz discovered Calculus independently at about the same time. It is also consistent with Bohm's conception of a universal flux.

In our search we are trying to use the mind and brain to perceive and understand the process of reality, both manifest and unmanifest.

Chopra[18] says,

"The brain has to adjust itself to any higher experience. It takes brain waves to turn the whirling, chaotic energy of the quantum soup into recognizable images and thoughts."

This is reminiscent of the conception of thought as 'a dance of the mind,' and makes it easy to see why we struggle to accommodate or integrate new insights, or energy configurations, into the patterns which are stored in the mind. It also illustrates why the development of knowledge evolves through the interaction of energy between particular mind, universal mind, brain and environment. The complex nature of the process makes it easy to understand why misperceptions and misconceptions arise in everyday life.

The concept of a universal flux/universal mind field which provides the potential for evolution is intriguing. If, indeed, mind fields do exist and are interactive, creativity could be conceived of as a process whereby an individual mind field interacts with the universal mind field to access the energy or potential for new, intuitive insight. If such possibilities exist it will be clear that any such interactions will not be precise or unambiguous and will be limited by the cognitive ability of the individual to process the energy and express the insight in terms of conceptual representation. We must not forget that thought does not provide a definitive, reflective picture of reality and is subject to change with changing perceptions.

We must not lose sight of the fact that feelings provide a barometer that is sensitive to intuition. What we call heart or gut feelings often provide reliable inner guidance in response to specific situations and we shall consider these in due course.

Reality and the Changing Forms in Nature and Thought

Each of us is aware of a flow of consciousness which is most apparent when the mind is still. This flow is broken by observations or thoughts which arise and catch our attention. Sometimes the thoughts slip away as quickly as they came, return to the mind and disappear from view. Sometimes these thoughts act as a trigger and bring to attention new thoughts by a process of association. When a thought arises, perhaps it interacts (as a result of brain activity) with conceptual structures stored within the flow of the mind. This, in turn, can lead to the arousal of thoughts which have conceptual links. For example, a person wakes up in the morning and thinks about making a cup of tea which he associates with taking his blood pressure tablet. If taking a tablet with his morning cup of tea has become a habit, surely it has become part of a conceptual framework related to the habit. The interaction between thoughts and concepts allows us to make plans and to organise our lives in an orderly way.

The process of understanding involves perceptions and thoughts relative to conceptual structures available to the mind. If we perceive that there is a correspondence or resonance between the thought and these underlying structures, this manifests itself as what we conceive to be the process of understanding and the thought seems reasonable. When thoughts or perceptions arise which do not resonate with our conceptual frameworks, then the reaction is one of puzzlement and lack of understanding. It seems to me that when this occurs there is an in-built propensity to re-establish the process of understanding, whereby brain and mind seek to match perceptions of reality, which are a function of the environment, to the conceptual frameworks stored in the mind field. What is sought is harmony between what is perceived to be reality and the cognitive structures which give meaning to this perceived reality. It is a search for unity and wholeness.

As our perceptions of reality change, the concepts in our mind evolve in an attempt to make sense of these perceptions. What we perceive to be 'truth' thus evolves and changes with our changing perceptions. It would appear that the mind is a function of the environment in which the individual is located and this provides a fertile source of experience and perceptions which feed the development of thoughts and concepts. Changes of experience and perception stimulate the brain/mind whose formative cause is to restore wholeness and unity.

When we experience a new perception, our brain attempts to match it (or associate it) to available conceptual structures and sometimes, by making minor adjustments to the framework, it is possible to assimilate the new information and restore understanding. However, there are occasions when observations or perceptions are so incompatible with conceptual patterns that it is not possible to assimilate them into existing frameworks.

If we accept that such systems as "particular mind" and "universal mind" exist, is it not possible that these could interact to facilitate a form of intelligent perception within the particular mind? This is not thought, in the accepted sense, but intuitive insight, and leads to a creative leap, inspired by a creative intelligence within the universal mind field. Furthermore, such intuitive insight may be preceded by heart or gut feelings inspired by some form of energy exchange between the universal flux and energy fields located in these areas of the body. Whatever the mechanisms may be which facilitate such changes, the outcome results in a new way of viewing the situation which introduces change to the conceptual frameworks. Understanding is restored in the form of a perception of unity between thought/observation and conceptual framework and may well be accompanied by a heart-felt sense of peace.

A match is restored between our perception of reality and theoretical insight, but this does not mean that our perceptions are accurate or that our theoretical insights are true. The adapted, or new concept is then stored within the flow of the mind-field until it is activated at some future date. Could it be that 'Eureka' moments, the heralds of profound creativity and revolutionary thinking, are the result of an interaction of mind fields: appertaining to the individual with the source of creative intelligence? Could it be that all forms of creativity have their origin in this type of phenomenon? As Bohm has intimated, man is not able to conceive 'reality as it is', all he has is theoretical insight which evolves with time.

Natural history tells us that nature is not a static creation which is standing still. Evolution is a concept that is well established and, no doubt, natural forms will change in the future, probably as a result of the built-in formative aspect of nature as it unfolds under the influence of environmental factors. Just as nature adapts and changes with the passage of time, so does the mind in the way it perceives and interprets reality. We are all aware of how nature endeavours to heal the body when it is injured or diseased and strives to restore it to health and wholeness. A similar process seems to operate within the troubled mind and soul, in so far as a creative intelligence seeks to restore wholeness of mind and unity of spirit when individuals open their hearts and minds to its influence.

In life we see that individuals have a wide range of interests, skills and competencies which, no doubt, relate to the degree of integration between body/brain/individual (particular) mind/universal mind. However, it is equally clear that even the most capable of individuals have only limited access to the creative intelligence of the universe. This is hardly surprising if we view the brain as a receiver or processor of a mind that is very inefficient and filters out much of the information which is accessible to it. Even so, I believe that each of us has the capacity to find inner wholeness, peace and harmony if we open our hearts and minds and allow our intuitive sixth sense to tune into the creative intelligence which is part of the "Ground of Being".

It seems to me that there is something in the depths of man's "being" which is pulling him towards a need for unity, wholeness and harmony. However, his awareness of this influence is masked by his misperceptions of reality which are influenced by unconscious forces that feed his illusory ego. Consequently, his personal prejudices, in addition to limitations of perception, present a picture of reality which is fragmented, lacks clarity and resembles the 'snowy' interference that accompanies poor reception on a television screen.

Fragmentation and Division

Bohm[19] says,

"Whenever men divide themselves from the whole of society and attempt to unite by identification within the group,

it is clear that the group must eventually develop internal strife, which leads to breakdown of its unity....True unity in the individual and between man and nature, as well as between man and man, can arise only in a form of action that does not attempt to fragment the whole of reality."

We have suggested that there is a formative nature in man which is directed toward the realisation of unity in body, mind and spirit. However, it would appear that in his quest for wholeness, he has allowed his brain to become a disruptive influence. His misperceptions of reality have led to a fragmentation of thought, whereby he relates to those who have similar ideas or opinions (or prejudices) and feels a bond which is a form of unity of mind.

At the same time, he creates a barrier between himself and those who hold different beliefs, and because his sense of "being" has become mind/brain-orientated he loses awareness of the spiritual bond he shares with them. His mind/brain (I use this combination to emphasise a lack of intuition) focuses on what he perceives to be difference and any potential common ground, through which bonds could be formed, is relegated in importance leading to a sense of polarisation and separation. The focus of his perception has been high-jacked and is forced to recognise difference rather than sameness. If he was able to stand back and gain a wider sense of perspective, he would see that the distinction between difference and sameness was blurred at the edges, depending on the focus of his perception. He may come to realise that the 'dance of the mind' which creates his thoughts is not a precise reflective image of reality but a hazy pointer towards some limited world-view (that it may indeed be prejudiced).

At a later date, he may become aware of new perceptions, causing him to question the validity of his conceptual framework and, through new insights, come to recognise that he has something in common with somebody initially perceived to be an adversary. How often do we see examples of politicians changing their allegiance, or of individuals 'converting' from one religion to another? It does not mean that they have suddenly gained an insight which has enabled them to see 'reality as it is'. It just means that what was initially perceived as a difference has been replaced by a perception of sameness. Furthermore, groups of 'like-minded' people rarely see eye-to-eye on everything and, sooner or later, issues arise which can polarise a group into different factions, a frequent happening within religious or political groups.

Could it be that part of the problem of fragmentation is the limitation of man's ability to take cognizance of the big picture in its entirety in one particular moment? His perceptions are split up into bite-sized pieces which he tries to digest but, in the process, he loses his capacity to maintain awareness of consistency between different areas of his conceptual frameworks. He is forced to struggle to pay attention to the different implications of different areas of thought in order to ensure that they are underpinned by a logical consistency which matches his perception of reality. Even then, his limited perceptions may well change with the passage of time, further undermining his confidence in the authenticity of the fixed concepts which form the foundations of his world view.

The challenge is to create a unified picture of reality in which all forms of thought inter-relate to form a coherent whole that is logically consistent and which resonates with what we intuitively feel to be the foundation of our whole "being" in body, mind and soul. This is impossible to do because when we access the mind we can temporarily lose cognizance of our awareness of spiritual "being" (soul) and become a separate "I", fragmented from the flow of universal "being" or "Being-itself". We can perceive ourselves to be thinkers of thoughts and, when we do this, the ego gains a foothold and it fragments our thinking. Changes in egotistic perceptions can play havoc with our conceptual frameworks causing them to fragment and wobble. This creates confusion which has a destabilizing effect on the individual and is part of the reason why the thoughts and beliefs of some people change with the weather and according to the company that they keep.

Until we recognise that man-made theories are purely models of reality and not reality itself we are going to continue to make the same mistake of fragmented thinking that will divide man against man. The question is, how do you get everybody to recognise that our theories are not 'descriptions of reality as it is' but ever-changing forms of insight which can point to, or indicate a reality that is implicit and not describable or specifiable in its totality?

Reality, Measurement and Values

Bohm[20] implies that the root cause of fragmentation may be linked to the concept of 'measure'. He suggests that, in the early phases of the development of civilisation, the word measure was used in the context of an internal quality which regulated the internal harmony of the individual. An awareness of the inner measure of things was seen to be the essential key to a healthy, happy, harmonious life. If somebody lost focus of this quality, which was not of necessity a conformation to some external standard, they lost a sense of integrity which affected their inner harmony causing fragmentation.

It appears to me that this quality was of an essence that wasn't rigidly defined by the mind but was a function of the soul and felt intuitively by the heart. It was a quality that acknowledged and valued the wholeness of the individual (in mind and soul) and the sense of unity with others. In my opinion, it was an acknowledgement or awareness of love as an underlying relatedness that embraces the essence of reality and leads to a view of life which does not measure according to external standards but responds to what is necessary in a specific situation.

Eastern wisdom has long recognised that reality is immeasurable with the brain/mind. It is impossible to measure, within the context of time, a phenomenon that is occurring in the "now" moment and is subject to change. One has to take cognizance of the fact that the reality of everyday living calls us to respond to different situations in ways which are appropriate and recognise a true sense of unity and brotherhood. Anything less will lead to fragmentation and inner disharmony.

Bohm[21] suggests that, with the passage of time, this notion of measure gradually began to change. Instead of being a subtle response to individual circumstances, leading to physical health, social order and mental harmony, it became a mechanical response that was influenced by the changing norms of society that prescribed external standards which became unconsciously accepted (e.g. the influence of fashion?). Man lost sight of the fact that measure is a form of insight which must, of necessity, embrace a perception of holism if it is to avoid fragmentation. Modern notions of measure have become rigid forms, determined by external standards imposed by society in general, leading to self-centred priorities which have divided society into groups and sub-groups.

In Western society the perception of reality is dominated by the preoccupation with measure in its myriad of prescribed and standardised forms (e.g. the fashion world's obsession with an extremely thin body as the ideal form). Many people have no idea what is of real value in life because they do not see measure as a form of insight which is internal to them, as something which resonates with the core of their "being". Their ability to perceive this is masked by the illusory demands of the ego which thrives on the confusion created by false standards and maintains its identity through the process of fragmentation. When our mind finally comes to accept that reality has its roots in unity and wholeness, that fragmentation is illusory, then, at that point the ego must die a death and disappear.

From the Eastern point of view, the primary reality is immeasurable and measure is an insight created by man. Bohm[22] makes an interesting point when he says,

"One may speculate that perhaps in ancient times, the men who were wise enough to see that the immeasurable is the primary reality were also wise enough to see that measure is insight into a secondary and dependent but nonetheless necessary aspect of reality. Thus they may have agreed with the Greeks that insight into measure is capable of helping to

bring about order and harmony in our lives, while at the same time, seeing perhaps more deeply, that it cannot be what is most fundamental in this regard".

This implies that, although reality is immeasurable, one has to live in the world in a way which gives order and meaning to life. In order for this to happen we have to be able to decide what is of value and this involves the concept of measure. We have to conceive of a system of measure which, although not synonymous with reality, resonates with it in a way that is felt within the depths of our soul. We have to define a baseline, a foundation on which to build a system of values. Furthermore, it will have to be one which we intuitively know to be true and of ultimate significance. Surely that truth must be that all creatures share a common state of "being" and are part of the unified whole of creation. The ultimate foundation of any system of measured values in human relationships must recognise this truth if, within the context of space and time, it is to give meaning to life in a way which is coincidental with immeasurable reality.

What Bohm[23] goes on to say is,

"What they (meaning wise men in the past) may further have said is that when measure is identified with the very essence of reality, this is illusion."

It seems to me that man has a problem here in so far as he has to live in the real world and this involves the identification of values (measure) which guide his behaviour. Reality is immeasurable so whatever values he chooses it is not possible to say definitely that they are coincidental with reality. Does this imply that whatever he does, his life is forced to be illusory and without substance? I think it means that he must respond intuitively to situations through heart-felt insight and must not respond from the perspective of his ego. He must choose his values wisely so that they promote unity rather than division and are under-pinned by love.

We have intimated that because reality cannot be defined by language, in terms of any fixed world-views, it will give rise to occasions where our paradigms appear inadequate and require a fresh, new approach. When this happens, ideas already contained within the whole field of measure prove to be inadequate and what is required is a new creative insight as an active response to creative intelligence. This is a function of unmanifest reality, the immeasurable, that is the formative cause of all that happens in the field of measure. When we open ourselves to creative intelligence, we set in motion a dynamic which facilitates intelligent perception to restore a level of understanding to dispel confusion.

Reality and Creative Intelligence

When you look at the animal kingdom you cannot but wonder at the power of its creation. It is unrealistic to think that this happened by chance and highly probable that there is a creative force, an aspect of the universal flux, which creates form and life. Paul Tillich calls this the "Ground of Being" ("Being-itself"), from which our "being" comes. This is a phenomenon which is intimately a part of who we are but, at the same time, extends beyond our physical form. It is both immanent and transcendent, a phenomenon which is both subject and object and therefore beyond description. We are part of the process of life which is an activity, not a thing, and therefore we are unable to capture the reality of this process in words.

I believe that life has been crafted by a creative intelligence which is accessible to man on a much reduced scale. We discussed earlier the possibility of individual mind fields and how these might interact with a universal mind field which is the source of creative intelligence. We also suggested that individual brains could show considerable variation in their capacity as both receiver and processor of mind, but that even the most receptive brains will be relatively inefficient and struggle to process intelligent information from what Chopra calls '*the whirling chaotic energy of quantum soup*'.

We see evidence of the changing forms of reality both in nature and the way life is lived on a day to day basis. History reveals the presence of evolutionary change in animal form and in the form of man's thinking and changing life styles. Access to creative intelligence has enabled him to invent tools and machines to make his life easier and rapid progress has been made since the advent of the industrial revolution. In more recent times, the invention of the silicon chip has led to the development of electronic gadgets which are developing at enormous pace.

When I was a child in the 1950's I can remember when my father bought our first television. It was amazing to watch John Wayne westerns or the FA Cup Final. The television was a box containing wires and electronic components which sat lifeless in the corner of the room on a table. However, when you plugged it in to the mains and turned on a switch it came to life with sound and pictures. On occasions, if one of its components failed it would break down, but once the part was repaired or replaced it was working again and as good as new. Eventually, with the passage of time, components would wear out and it would break down too frequently. Its useful life would be over and it would be discarded and replaced by a new model.

Twenty years after watching that first black and white television, with a twelve inch screen, I bought my first colour television. How different it was, much bigger with a screen twice the size, a remote control and far more sophisticated electronics. Five years ago I bought a model with a forty inch screen which is connected to a Sky box and satellite dish. I am now able to choose from a multitude of channels, record more than one programme at the same time or even put the TV programme on pause while I make a cup of tea. The modern television looks very different to its predecessors and has changed with the development of more sophisticated components. Modern machines are controlled by artificial intelligence in the form of computers which can be programmed to respond to different circumstances. Computers can perform some tasks more quickly and efficiently than a person but this form of intelligence is limited and, at this present point in time, does not have access to the same level of creativity as a human brain.

Man's ability to access creativity has evolved and will, no doubt, continue to do so until he becomes extinct. He has invented and developed a vast range of different types of machine, all of which have undergone a process of evolution. However, man's ability to interact with creative intelligence in his development of technology cannot compare with the level of intelligence that created man himself. Machines need energy to bring them to life but then become lifeless when the source of energy is switched off. What is the source of the energy, the life force which gives animation to man and sustains him until the point of death?

Reality and Being

When we think about the essence of life we are thinking about something which is abstract and impossible to define. It has been suggested that unmanifest reality may be conceived as a universal flux of energy which gives rise to changing forms. Could it be that this phenomenon is responsible for the creation of living creatures composed of complex, inter-related energy fields, which exist as a consequence of a life-force that manifests itself in what we have called "being"? This life force or energy, referred to as spirit, would not be an individual phenomenon but would be all-embracing and arise from a source ("Being-itself") within the universal flux which is the "Ground of Being".

When we use terms such as "being", "Being-itself", or "Ground of Being" it must be emphasised that we have no absolute knowledge of such phenomena. We are seeking to give concrete expression to something we sense intuitively but cannot perceive in terms of our physical senses. We are only able to do this in terms of metaphorical expression which creates models or art forms which attempt to match our perceptions of reality.

The best way I can view this abstract notion of "being" is to think in terms of the energy we call electricity that we use to power our homes, and to draw an analogy between this and the essence of our human form. Each of our homes receives a supply of energy, in the form of electricity, which we use to provide lighting or give power and life to various machines and tools which we have at our disposal. This is analogous to the energy of "being" that gives life to our human form. The electricity supply to each of our households is the same (just as "being" is common to all of us) and comes from a high energy source (cf. "Being-itself") which is founded in the National Grid (cf. the "Ground of Being" in the Universal Flux). This metaphor breaks down when you consider the National Grid does not provide an endless supply of electricity, and the universal flux may be considered to be of infinite proportions. One may also argue that our bodies need another source of energy to nourish and sustain their physical form. Nevertheless, it presents a hazy picture which, in spite of its limitations, may help us to gain some concrete conception of the unknown.

Electricity is capable of generating energy fields and it is conceivable that "being" may generate a field of consciousness and a non-localised mind field that are subject to the brain's control. A combination of mind, brain and spirit could exert an influence over the behaviour of the inter-penetrating energy systems within the body and affect its behaviour. When consciousness is not distracted by thought and the mind is 'empty', we are aware of our spirit, our real essence as "being" which we perceive as a sense of presence. If we are in a meditative state and the mind is still, we become aware of our breathing and are conscious of the fact that we are living, that we exist. We experience what we call a sense of "being" (from the verb "to be") and what we sense is a process, a form of activity not a thing.

Sam Harris[24], who has a doctorate in neuroscience, says that most scientists believe that our mental and spiritual lives are wholly dependent upon the workings of our brain and that, when the brain dies, the stream of our "being" must come to an end. The truth is that we simply don't know what happens after death. The idea that brains produce consciousness is open to question and there are reasons to believe that science will be unable to prove or disprove it.

"Being" can be viewed as a process that has various dimensions that work together holistically. There is the physical, bodily form activated by a spiritual, biological life force with a related dimension of mind. What appears to be the case is that human beings are complex energy systems and the abstract concepts which we refer to as mind, spirit and soul are closely linked to the concepts of consciousness and "being". Our understanding is imprecise and incomplete because the process of thought is indefinite. Our brain is looking to present a sharp, clearly focused picture of hidden phenomena but our conceptions are vague and fuzzy. They are shrouded in fog because our limited powers of perception are unable to perceive reality as it is.

If we are not careful, we forget the importance of feelings and give greater significance to thought that is the product of brain activity. It is conceivable that different areas of the body are associated with energy fields which impact on our sense of "being" and mind. What we refer to as "heart-felt feelings", are associated with love and compassion and are generally experienced or felt in the region of the body where the heart is located. Could it be that an energy field related to the heart is able to interact with the universal flux in a way which facilitates intuitive perception?

Our capacity to feel is something which we experience in the "now" moment (they are present feelings) whereas our thinking can be locked into thoughts of the past or fears of the future. One could argue that feelings can be evoked by memories or thoughts about the future. However, when the mind is empty and there is a synchronicity between our spiritual "being" and the universal flux, there is a form of communication which occurs in the moment. This can express itself in terms of feelings and thought which is not the product of time-related thought or reason but a form of direct perception which we call intuitive insight. New insights appear to come from nowhere and these, in conjunction with the mind, are translated into forms of behaviour that seem to by-pass the usual thought processes of the brain. We do not understand the unconscious mechanisms that facilitate such communication, or the role, if any, played by the brain.

It would appear that the energy fields associated with the heart and brain exert a huge influence over the way we behave. The brain is capable of both rational and irrational behaviour and is often unable to determine the difference between the two, whereas, the heart is more sensitive and able to sense and make use of intuitive feelings to create a different perspective. In order to live in a rational way there is clearly a need to cultivate an awareness of both heart and brain in the way we make decisions as they both influence the workings of the mind.

The inter-relationship between the "Ground of Being", "universal mind" and "being" might be represented diagrammatically as follows Figure 2.2:

Ground of Being (Universal Flux)

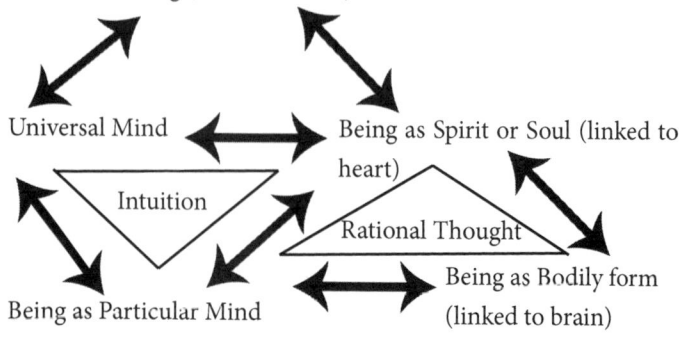

Universal Mind ⟷ Being as Spirit or Soul (linked to heart)

Intuition

Rational Thought

Being as Particular Mind ⟷ Being as Bodily form (linked to brain)

Could it be that when the mind is empty of thought, consciousness becomes conscious of itself and its relationship to the universal flux? When this happens, is it not conceivable that this could lead to synchronicity between the energy fields which give form to the individual, and the universal flux itself, with a related exchange of energy and information? Could it be that this, in turn, leads to a sense of harmony and a reassuring conviction of what the individual must do in a particular situation? Furthermore, is this process of consciousness being conscious of itself, what we mean when we talk about 'soul awareness'?

This process takes place when the particular mind is empty of thought and man is free of psychological time. The individual becomes conscious of the spiritual dimension, in touch with his soul, and experiences the effect of "Being-itself" upon his own "being". This manifests itself as a peaceful presence and is a positive, life-enhancing experience. However, individuals who are cut off from "Being-itself", and in the grip of their own ego, create a negative form of energy which can lead to states of mind which embrace the depths of despair, or are capable of perpetrating what we call evil.

Body, mind and spirit, as aspects of "being", interact to give us a sense of who we are as people and contribute to the health and general sense of well-being of an individual. The relationship between particular mind/universal mind/spirit is a function of soul awareness and inspires intuitive communication through a combination of heart and mind. This can easily be lost when the brain becomes too dominant.

If the biological functioning of the body is destroyed by malnutrition, disease, injury or through natural causes, the individual dies and ceases "to be" in natural terms. We do not know what happens at the point of death to the life force or spirit which gave the individual a sense of "being". This may continue to exist as a separate energy system in a different dimension or may return to the "Ground of Being" or universal flux. Spiritual mediums suggest that we do not cease to exist when we die and that death is the gateway to a new form of existence. I suppose that we shall not learn the truth until we die, but personally, I feel that this is not an issue to be considered in depth. Our primary concern is to live in such a way as appears meaningful in terms of our current temporal existence.

When we look at the world today it is abundantly clear that many people do not enjoy a meaningful existence. In some cases, individuals have such a low sense of "being" that they wish to end their lives. These are people whose minds are troubled, whose spiritual centre is so empty that life has no sense of direction. Why is it that some human beings are able to live with a full sense of well-being and inner peace, whilst many are unhappy and experience a life-style without meaning and thus despair? Tillich would have suggested that the answer was related to the existence of "non-being".

Non-Being

Paul Tillich[25] says,

"The ground of everything that is, is not a dead identity without movement and becoming; it is living creativity. Creatively it affirms itself, eternally conquering its own non-being."

He suggests that "being" and "non-being" are abstract

concepts that cannot be defined literally and can only be discussed metaphorically. He says that "being" has "non-being" within itself, as that which is eternally present and eternally overcome in the process of the divine life. Although "being" and "non-being" may be abstract terms, perhaps it is possible to gain a vague idea of how they relate to life in general.

What could we mean by "non-being"? We have suggested that "being" has biological, cognitive and spiritual dimensions which interact and contribute to the wholeness and well-being of the individual. Could it be that "being" is a positive, life-affirming energy or vitality, whereas "non-being" is a form of negative energy, which is a drain on life and changes the nature of our energy systems? In biological terms, "non-being" could be regarded as a drain on the life force leading eventually, to physical decline, death and decay; cognitively it could be part of a process of negativity that embraces concepts like fear, envy, guilt and self-condemnation; and spiritually it could be a manifestation of emptiness and meaninglessness.

When Tillich talks about living creativity, it draws to mind a vitality that embraces a positive, life-enhancing form of energy which leads to evolution within the physical, psychological and spiritual dimensions of life. This can be seen in the situation whereby microbes mutate and change in order to survive in the presence of antibiotics, or rats develop an immunity to rat poison. This reality, which Tillich calls living creativity, or the ground of everything, is that which tries to overcome the negative element, called "non-being" that leads to death and despair.

I believe that there is a dynamic relationship between the phenomena which Tillich refers to as "being" and "non-being". I visualise this as being similar to the dynamic equilibrium that exists in a chemical reaction between reactants and products:

$$\text{Reactants} \rightleftharpoons \text{Products}$$

$$A + B \rightleftharpoons C + D$$

By altering the conditions under which the reaction is carried out you can influence the equilibrium of the reaction. If you choose favourable reaction conditions you can ensure a better yield of products and push the equilibrium to the right.

$$A + B \rightleftharpoons C + D$$

However, if the conditions are wrong the reaction may not take place at all, or the yield of products will be very low.

Similarly I foresee a dynamic equilibrium between "being" and "non-being".

$$\text{Being} \rightleftharpoons \text{Non-being}$$

I believe that the position of the equilibrium can be influenced by different conditions, by our level of conscious or unconscious behaviour. When our level of conscious awareness is high (or we live beyond the constraints of psychological time) the equilibrium is pushed to the left.

$$\text{Being} \rightleftharpoons \text{Non-being} \dots\dots\dots(1)$$

When our level of conscious awareness is low (we are preoccupied with psychological time) and we live unconsciously, the equilibrium is forced to the right

$$\text{Being} \rightleftarrows \text{Non-being} \quad\quad (2)$$

In both situations there are elements of "being" and "non-being", we never reach a stage where either is completely eliminated (while we are physically alive).

Another analogy which illustrates the dynamic relationship between "being" and "non-being" is the flow of electricity in an electrical circuit with a variable resistance.

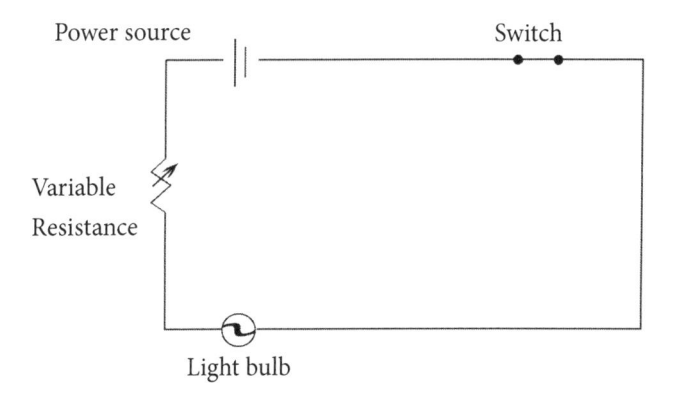

Figure 2.3

When the circuit is switched on electricity begins to flow around the circuit. If the resistance is set at a high value, its flow is restricted and the current has a low value but if the resistance is gradually reduced the flow of current gradually increases. There is a dynamic relationship between the current and the resistance.

$$\text{Current (I)} \propto 1/\text{Resistance (R)}$$

As we have already suggested, it would seem that the total phenomenon of "being" embraces a number of elements including body, mind and spirit and that our mind is unable to appreciate the complexity of the issue. However, if we turn our attention to the aspects of mind (or more specifically brain-dominated activity of mind) and spirit (in terms of intuitive behaviour) it seems to me that the behaviour of an electric circuit is illustrative of the dynamic relationship between "being" and "non-being".

Perhaps there is a creative, intelligent form of energy within the universe, "Being-itself" which is the source of life and "being". Perhaps man is conscious of this phenomenon during the process we have called soul awareness and feels a resonance and sense of unity with it. In our analogy, we will assume that the creative energy, "Being-itself", is analogous to the power source and from it flows the current of spiritual "being".

The variable resistance in our circuit is the brain-dominated, false sense of self, known as the ego which operates through a lack of conscious awareness within psychological time (we shall discuss this concept in more depth in the next chapter). Its value varies according to the level of ego participation in the behaviour of the individual and it has a wide range of values. The other components in the circuit include the switch, left in the 'on' position during the natural life of the individual, and the connecting wires and the light bulb, which we will consider to have negligible resistance.

```
       Power source              Switch
       (Being-itself)          (Life connection)
```

Variable Resistor

(Ego)

Light bulb

(Spiritual centre)

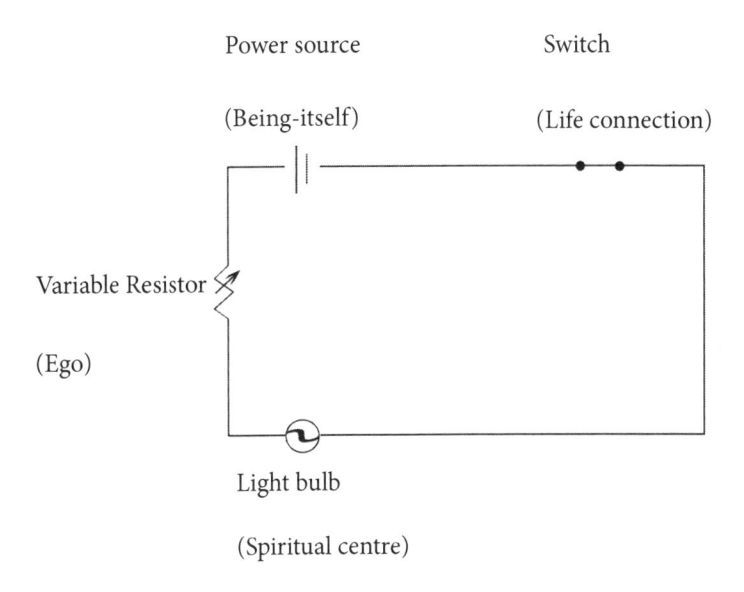

Figure 2.4

When an individual is in a state of soul awareness he experiences a sense of connection with the universal flux and there is a feeling of peace, harmony and unity with no sense of separation. Ego involvement is negligible, the resistance to spiritual energy in the circuit of his life is very low and, just like an electric circuit with a low resistance, the current of spiritual being is strong, flows freely in his life and the light in his 'circuit' (the joy, peace, love, serenity, concern and care, in his heart) shines brightly for all to see. One could say that, like Jesus or the Buddha he becomes a guiding light and a shining example for others to follow. The dynamic equilibrium between "being" and "non-being" is orientated strongly in favour of "being".

Conversely, when an individual loses soul awareness and is preoccupied with the concerns of the ego, it is likely that he will not be at peace with himself because he is resisting the flow of spiritual energy. Furthermore, there is a possibility that he will not be at peace with other people from whom he will feel a sense of separation. The degree of alienation or estrangement will be proportional to the level of intensity of ego involvement and may vary from a sense of mild irritation to intense hatred or evil intent. The ego behaves like a variable resistance which suppresses the flow of spiritual energy and when the level of ego intensity is high, the light in his 'circuit' is unable to shine (there is no love in his heart) and generates no warmth or light. The dynamic equilibrium's orientation is strongly in favour of "non-being".

I believe it is the false sense of self, or "ego", that is what Tillich refers to as psychological and spiritual "non-being". The ego is an illusion that separates the individual from the "Ground of Being" and the "being" of his fellow man. It is a brain-centred creation which operates within what has been referred to as psychological time.

Summary of Key Ideas

- Reality can be conceived as a flowing process of universal flux (energy) that leads to the creation of matter, nature and thought. The process is not static but in a state of constant change.
- Reality consists of what is both manifest and unmanifest.
- Man's perceptions of reality are restricted by the limited capacity of his sense receptors, and his brain which acts as a filter.
- Manifest reality is perceived through the five senses

but unmanifest reality can only be perceived by a sixth sense, an aspect of consciousness which is perceived in the eternal "now" and gives rise to intuitive insight.
- Thought is a 'dance of the mind' which does not provide a definitive, reflective picture of reality but a hazy, foggy impression, subject to change with changing perceptions. It is a way of looking at reality but not a 'true copy of reality as it is.' Words act as pointers and can be used as a tool to give a superficial picture of manifest reality.
- Meaning is established through conceptual frameworks, or paradigms (theories) which resonate with man's perceptions. Perceptions can change in the light of experience and conceptual frameworks need to adapt or change radically to maintain coherence and understanding.
- Man's knowledge of the world changes through insights which find expression in terms of new conceptual frameworks or paradigms.
- Nature is imbued with a life force or energy that is grounded in the universal flux and gives rise to what we call "being", or the essence of life.
- We appear to be aware of a connection between the energy of what we call our "being" and the energy of the universal flux. We refer to this connection as soul awareness and it is perceived through a sixth sense
- Human beings are made of complex, interacting energy systems and the concepts which we refer to as mind, spirit and soul are impossible to express

definitively, but inter-related to the equally vague concepts of consciousness and being. The imprecision of thought leaves us groping in the dark like a blind man reaching for objects that he senses are there but cannot see.

- The reality we experience is a function of how different energy systems, within the body and the environment, interact with each other and universal mind. The outcome leads to inner harmony or disharmony.
- Mind can be conceived as an energy field, capable of storing information or memory in the form of immaterial energy which can be drawn into consciousness and processed through the agency of a physical brain.
- The universal flux could give rise to a universal mind field which could be the source of creative energy. Creativity could be conceived as a process whereby an individual mind field interacts with the universal mind field to access the energy or potential for new, intuitive insight.
- If such possibilities exist it will be clear that any such interactions will not be precise or unambiguous and will be limited by the cognitive ability of the individual to process the energy and express the insight in terms of conceptual representation.
- Love is a form of synchronous resonance or interaction between the life energy or spirit (spiritual energy) of the individual with the "Ground of Being" ("Being itself" or the universal flux) or with that of other individuals. It is a sense of relativity to a shared participation in the process of being, or the

acknowledgement of a shared essence.
- Values are a form of measure that can be made with the heart or the brain. Authentic values are inner values with their origin in the heart and soul, that work in tandem with the mind. Inauthentic values are brain-driven responses related to the separate 'I' or psychological time.
- There appears to be a natural propensity in nature to restore wholeness in body, mind and spirit.
- "Being-itself" is a positive, creative, life-enhancing form of energy within the universal flux leading to evolution within the physical, psychological and spiritual dimensions of life. This reality is caught up in a dynamic relationship with "non-being", a negative influence, affecting the energy fields within the body.
- The identification of the ego seen as our sense of self is the source of irrational, fragmented thought, leading to psychological and spiritual "non-being". This operates within "psychological time".

CHAPTER 3.

Psychological Time

The Nature of Psychological Time and its Relationship to Chronological Time

During the course of our lives, each of us is faced with numerous, potentially problematic situations and how we deal with them will have a large bearing on whether the outcome leads to harmony or conflict. Why is it that some people cause disharmony wherever they go whilst others exude a calm peaceful presence? Maybe the answer has something to do with what Krishnamurti called psychological time. Psychological time comes into operation when a person is conscious of himself as a separate entity and creates an illusion of subject and object, whereby the individual (an 'I'), reflecting on a specific situation, has turned himself into an object (a 'me').

In Chapter 1 we talked about consciousness and the illusion of subject/object duality. Let us see how this relates to psychological time.

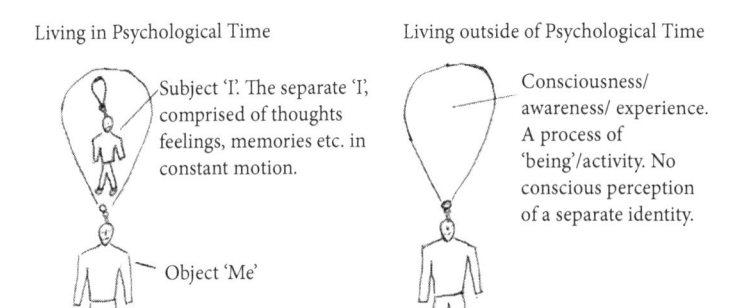

Living in Psychological Time	Living outside of Psychological Time
Subject 'I'. The separate 'I', comprised of thoughts feelings, memories etc. in constant motion. Object 'Me'	Consciousness/ awareness/ experience. A process of 'being'/activity. No conscious perception of a separate identity.

Figure 3.1

Earlier, we considered consciousness, the thing you call "I", as really a stream of experiences, sensations, thoughts, memories and feelings in constant motion, giving the impression that 'I' is something of substance. In reality, it is an illusory, changeable self-image dependent on our psychological make-up at any one given time. Sometimes 'I' can be confident whilst at other times lacks confidence, or it can feel the life and soul of the party or morose and depressed. We often fail to recognise that, in reality, each person is not an isolated object but a flowing process (of "being"), not static and with no specific identity other than the essence of our "being". Our brain reflects on, or re-lives, past experiences as if they were part of the present and spends time worrying about future happenings. This form of thought leads to a projection or desire for certain outcomes, attachment to which causes fear, anxiety, disappointment and conflict. If man is to be able to live in a way free from inner conflict, psychological time must come to an end and he must learn to adapt his life to chronological time.

How does psychological time differ from chronological time? Psychological time is a process that involves both memory and imagination which invokes both the past and future within the present moment. Consequently, conscious awareness of the present moment is lost in a preoccupation with past happenings, or concerns over future happenings. While this is occurring, time moves slowly but inexorably. Nobody can stop this process which provides the backdrop to our journey through life, from cradle to the grave. As the ravages of time take their toll we can observe continuous physical changes. Part of us remains unchanged however, and that is our perception of "being". This is time-less and we see it to be the same whether we are twenty or sixty years old, but we are only conscious of it when psychological time has ended and we are totally absorbed in the "now" moment of chronological time.

When psychological time is absent our mind is either still or concentrating on the task in hand, whether this involves a craftsman's skill or a sportsperson's total absorption in sport. His "being" flows with the activity in the eternal "now" moment as he becomes involved, and he loses all cognizance of his own personal identity which is now associated with the skill he is using. When he is operating at the highest level, his movements are spontaneous and often beyond thought as his actions are guided by an in-built intelligence or skill. When we are totally absorbed in purposeful activity, we live outside psychological time, lose track of chronological time which then appears 'to fly', and we experience the joy of living or the joy of "being". Conversely, if we become too preoccupied with egotistic concerns and caught up in psychological time, the anxieties, fears, disappointments and conflict take away the joy of living. We lose our awareness of the joy of "being" which is only manifested when our illusory ego has disappeared and we are living fully in the present moment.

The Nature of Rational and Irrational Thought and Behaviour

When you are conscious of "being" you are not aware of the past or future but of the reality of who you are. This reality is timeless (in terms of psychological time) but must exist in the "now" moment of chronological time. When you live in the 'being mode' you are not influenced by psychological time. Your mind operates outwardly under the influence of intelligent perception which can shape your thought in a rational way.

Building on what we discussed in Chapter 2, this could be expressed diagrammatically as follows Figure 3.2:

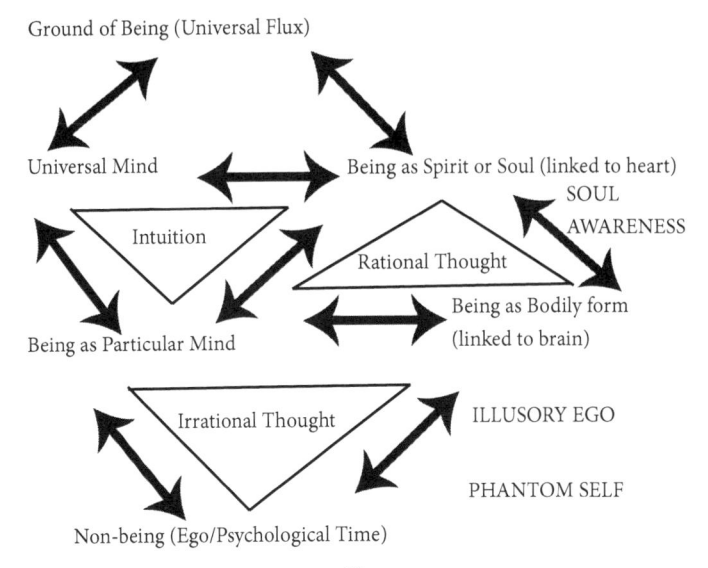

Ground of Being (Universal Flux)

Universal Mind ↔ Being as Spirit or Soul (linked to heart)

SOUL AWARENESS

Intuition

Rational Thought

Being as Bodily form (linked to brain)

Being as Particular Mind

Irrational Thought

ILLUSORY EGO

PHANTOM SELF

Non-being (Ego/Psychological Time)

When we use the word 'rational' we tend to use it in the context of conscious, reasoned thought or behaviour. However, the dictionary does suggest that the word is applicable to something 'based on or conforming to what can be tested by reason'. In view of this, is it possible for intuition, which is not based on reasoned argument, to be considered a rational process?

Rational thought is not thought that captures reality as it is. We have already established that this is not possible. Rational thought appears to be that which recognises the illusory nature of psychological time and tries to function under the influence of intuitive, intelligent perception and reason. The rational mind recognises the interconnectedness of all life and acts from the perspective of love, a natural consequence of the unity felt with the "Ground of Being". Furthermore, the rational mind is never dogmatic because it realises that knowledge is relative, not absolute, and is in the process of evolving. Truth can only be perceived in the eternal "now" because its perception may change with the passage of time. I believe that the rational mind operates in a state whereby universal mind and soul work together in tandem with the brain, to influence the particular mind in a way which by-passes psychological time and egotistic thought. It accesses insight, born of creative intelligence with a moderating and transformative effect on the thought process.

How does this happen? Krishnamurti[1] suggests that the brain is a function of time whereas the mind is independent of time. Could it be that, during moments of soul awareness, when the mind is empty of thought in the "now" moment (i.e. the brain is not engaged in conscious thought), the particular mind and soul experience synchronicity with the universal flux? If this is the case, could they experience a degree of connectivity with the universal flux that facilitates an interaction between our brain, particular mind and universal mind? Does this lead to an intuitive response, the result of the perception of a creative intelligence within the universal mind field that operates within the 'now' moment beyond conscious thought that is a product of time?

If such a process is possible, could it take the form of direct perception, a spontaneous response which by-passes the normal thought process and avoids the pitfalls of psychological time? If this is the case, what part, if any, will be played by the brain? It will be an unconscious process, not based on conscious, reasoned argument, so how can we know whether or not it is rational? If the brain has a part to play in intuitive insight, can we be certain that the outcome will lead to rational behaviour of a spiritual origin that is authentic and free of the instincts that drive the ego? We have suggested that all thought and knowledge is 'a dance of the mind', a pointer to reality that cannot capture and define it in its totality, and so I suppose the honest answer is that we do not know for certain.

In view of what we have just said, and the levels of uncertainty relating to all forms of knowledge, is there any way we may discover whether or not our thought or behaviour is rational? I believe that Bohm[2] has given us a clue when he suggests that it can be possible to abstract some level of understanding guiding one's actions in relation to a thing or situation so the outcome is harmonious and consistent with cognitive apprehension.

If intuitive thought is rational it will generally promote action directed toward the attainment of some unity of "being" between the individual, his fellow man and the

"Ground of Being". This will be sensed as a heart-felt resonance within the individual's soul, an inner conviction of the rational authenticity of an action founded in love. If genuine intuition does lead to 'reasonable behaviour' should it be considered as rational, or would the terms 'pre-logical' or 'pre-rational' be more appropriate? We shall return to this question later when we consider man's quest for meaning.

One may argue that many issues that arise within the context of living can be complex and require detailed thought and planning for resolution. Furthermore, they are issues which are impossible to resolve to the satisfaction of all interested parties and so, whatever the outcome it is bound to involve a conflict of interests. Whatever course of action is taken will lead to polarised opinions and a state of disunity. This is a realistic scenario of many situations occurring in everyday life and certainly solutions do not always present themselves spontaneously.

When this happens one might argue that the rational response would be to take no immediate action, if a viable option. It is the spontaneous, intuitive response of wisdom that recognises that a process of reflection or discussion is necessary. When it is apparent that there is no immediate answer, it is prudent to delay making a decision and to allow time for creative intelligence and universal mind to suggest a way forward at a later date. This approach eventually leads to an intuitive feeling that a particular course of action is appropriate. The individual is left with a sense of inner reassurance and conviction about the authenticity of the decision, even though there is a sense of realisation that there will be individuals who will be less than happy with the outcome. We live in a world in which psychological time is a key player and consequently, many problems will appear insoluble. It is inevitable that those individuals who are trapped in psychological time will experience the dissonance which accompanies egotistical concerns.

Krishnamurti[3] believes that there is an immense source of energy within the universe which we could use to solve our problems. He says[4],

"Tentatively, there is something in us that is operating, there is something in us...much greater."

If the universal flux is the source of everything, it must be the source of energy to which Krishnamurti refers. He is perhaps saying that we can perceive reality in a more authentic way than is possible just through conscious brain activity. Man's normal thought processes access the particular mind through the brain, which diminishes his awareness of universal mind and spirit. When this happens his brain is inclined to create the illusion of a separate entity, casting a shadow over his soul awareness. Such activity cuts off access to the creative intelligence and wisdom of universal mind and his particular mind can become entangled in irrational thought within the process of psychological time. Consequently he is unable to make use of the creative energy of the universe. Conversely, when he is in a state of soul awareness he is conscious of a 'presence' which transcends him. Krishnamurti might say, *"something in him is operating…much greater".*

Krishnamurti appears to be suggesting that man is able to access a phenomenon which gives him a far greater sense of personal power than is possible solely through conscious brain activity. This power is accessed through the process of unconscious intuition. He must learn to recognise that conscious thought may be subject to an irrational influence that comes about through another form of unconscious brain activity, attributable to an illusory phantom. If thought is to be rational it needs to be cognizant of these two influences and blend conscious thought with intuition.

Man appears to live in harmony with the universe when his consciousness is conscious of itself and he experiences what we described previously as soul awareness. Could it be the case that disharmony occurs when his consciousness has given itself a phantom? This illusion is the source of man's insecurity and fears and is responsible for his irrational thinking and behaviour, as it flounders in the sea of psychological time, searching to find that something which will give it security and a sense of significance.

When this happens man looks in on himself and uses all his energy to protect this illusory identity which he perceives to be all-important. In so-doing, could it be that his natural energy frequencies are changed in a way in which they no longer resonate with the universal flux, creating a state which manifests disharmony and conflict? Does it not make sense for man to look outward and seek unity with others through love, and in so-doing does he not align his natural energy with the universal flux and create harmony? Is this not the manifestation of rational behaviour?

Psychological Time and its Relationship to lack of Conscious Awareness and Genetic Predisposition

When man is consciously-aware of his "being" he senses a connection with the "Ground of Being" and the "being" of his fellow man. He feels in his heart that unity is a foundation of reality. This is something he feels in the depths of his "being", it is something he knows intuitively, an insight which is beyond conscious thought. However, in spite of this, he appears unable to sustain a permanent awareness of this reality and his brain frequently undermines this conviction during the process of psychological time. Maybe this whole issue is a function of the dynamic equilibrium between "being" and "non-being", of brain and heart.

$$\text{Being} \rightleftharpoons \text{Non-being}$$

$$\text{Heart (soul)} \rightleftharpoons \text{Brain (Ego)}$$

$$\text{Unity} \rightleftharpoons \text{Disunity (Conflict)}$$

$$\text{Intuition} \rightleftharpoons \text{Psychological knowledge}$$

Having gained an insight into the problem, how do we maintain the necessary level of conscious-awareness to prevent the intrusion of the ego? How do we maintain a situation whereby the dynamic equilibrium in each of the examples above is pushed to the left and kept there? A factor appears to draw the attention of man to the separate existence of his physical body, as perceived by his physical senses, and the identity of this with his illusory ego. This appears to have its roots in the struggle for survival which conditions his mind and holds it in this pattern. This dynamic relationship between "being" and "non-being" appears to be connected to a genetic predisposition to struggle and survive.

Pre-historic necessity resulted in the evolution of man's brain, conscious as he was of the need to survive in a hostile environment, aware of the threats to his life. The process of evolution heightened this awareness and honed his survival skills. The developing awareness of self-consciousness resulted in a 'self' concept which he related to his physical form. This developing spiritual awareness of "being" was given an illusory, individual focus (ego) by the brain in conjunction with the mind, and the realisation of his true spiritual nature, as a universal phenomenon, was masked or hidden.

This misperception seemed to become part of his genetic inheritance and was passed on through the generations. It created a blind spot whereby he is unable to recognise the nature of his "being" as a universal phenomenon. It is the predisposition of the brain/particular mind to fiercely defend the illusory ego, and the drive to preserve its identity, which is the root cause of man's irrationality.

The problem is that the aggressive, competitive characteristics needed to ensure man's survival in the past have not adapted to the needs of modern-day living. There is really no need for anybody in the world to die of malnutrition or hyperthermia and our safety is not threatened by wild animals, so hence there is no need for conflict of any description. Instead of being able to enjoy his ability to provide for his basic needs and live a peaceful, stress-free life, he has created a whole range of artificial needs which he now regards as essential.

In order to meet these needs he works long hours in a competitive environment with his attention focused on the 'having mode', stressed out, disillusioned and unaware of the 'being mode' of living which is the only true path to peace, joy and contentment. All he has done is channelled his aggression from competing with animals in the wild, to competing with his fellow-man, either through wars or in the work place. During the past century man has endured two senseless, bloody world wars, numerous smaller conflicts and, but for the threat of nuclear conflict, would no doubt have seen more carnage.

He needs to realise that the conception of a separate 'I' may have been useful in the past in the quest for survival but it has now served its useful purpose. He will continue to be irrational unless he comes to the realisation that who he believes himself to be is an illusion. The query then faced is one of identity. If he is not his ego, who is he, because this is the only identity he seems able to recognise? He has to live within the context of chronological time and utilize his brain/mind facility in a rational way that will eliminate a perception of 'me,' or what we have called psychological time. However, psychological time is surreptitious and invades our thought processes like a virus unless we are able to maintain a high level of conscious awareness of our real identity as "being".

Man's brain now needs to evolve in order to recognise the illusion it has created and to appreciate the damaging effect this has on relationships and on the potential for harmony and peace. He needs to become aware of a perception of 'self' which lies beyond subject/object duality. This we will discuss later when we consider what it means to be oneself.

The Disproportionate Significance given to Psychological Knowledge

Knowledge, in all its forms, appears to be an attempt by the mind to grasp the nature of reality. Certain types of knowledge appear to acquire disproportionate significance in the psyche and stupefy the brain by taking on a form of absolute, instead of relative importance. Why is it that intelligent people find it difficult to break out of the groove carved out by psychological knowledge? Bohm[5] suggests that it is because this knowledge creates the 'me', and the 'me' is the experience of an entity, an illusory state of "being" which seems not to be of knowledge but of some real "being" (it seems to have substance). This illusion has great power which conditions man's thinking.

Bohm[6] makes a very interesting observation, in so far as you can explain the principle of psychological knowledge to a person who may well understand intellectually what you are trying to say. However, if his status is threatened, he sees this as a threat to his whole "being", it doesn't appear that he is dealing with knowledge, but something much more. For example, an actor may become extremely upset by a critical review of his latest film. His personal perception as being a fine actor is a strong feature of his self-image (or ego) and is seriously hurt by the criticism. The knowledge that his performance has not been well-received by the critic is given disproportionate significance by the psyche of the actor, seen as a threat to his status as an actor or his self-image. This is magnified out of proportion because he perceives this to be a threat to his real 'self' and does not realise that all that is threatened is his illusory ego.

Bohm says,

"At first sight knowledge seems to be passive, which you could use if you wanted to, and which you could just put aside if you wished, which is the way it should be...But then the moment comes when knowledge no longer appears to be knowledge."

When this happens, the thought process becomes

distorted or disordered by the perceptions of an illusory centre or entity controlling the decision-making process. What in fact happens is that knowledge, generally considered passive but really active, works outside our process of awareness and acts in a way which is distorted by psychological time and disrupts the order of the brain. Returning to the example of our actor, the knowledge of his unfavourable review may preoccupy his thoughts within the context of psychological time. He may feel the criticism unjustified and will seek to get his revenge on the critic at some future date. Alternatively, he may feel that the critical review is heralding the demise of his career and turn to drink, or commit suicide. Whatever the outcome, his knowledge of what, after all, was somebody's opinion, has been given disproportionate attention by the ego and responded to in an irrational manner.

Psychological Time and its relationship to Love

It is my conviction that the reality of spiritual "being" finds expression in love, whereas the particular mind, under the brain's influence gets drawn into a pattern of thought that fragments or separates. The brain appears to have evolved in a way that, by necessity, filters out large aspects of reality, and selectively focuses on factors which promote the security and interests of its own person, and those to whom it is attached. I specifically use the word 'attached', rather than love, for I believe the true nature of love is a function of spiritual "being". The special relationship we experience with those to whom we feel a very close bond is not dissociated from thought, and is therefore the result of a mixture of different factors which may, or may not involve love.

If love is an acknowledgement of, and a commitment to shared "being", it cannot be primarily a relationship to a specific person, and must be a general orientation of relatedness of a person to the world as a whole. If an individual loves only one other person and is unconcerned about the rest of his fellow men, his love is not love but an enlarged form of ego attachment. Love recognises our shared spiritual essence, and in a perfect world we would all relate to each other as equals in the 'dance of life', but as we have already conceded, this is not what we perceive in reality. The existence of "non-being" ensures that Utopia does not exist and the concept of love has been fragmented, through psychological time, into different perceived forms, each one coloured by human thought and emotion. Indeed the Greeks have different words to signify for different forms of love, suggesting love is a spiritual reality that is impossible to define in psychophysical terms.

Fromm[7] suggests, and I agree, that love, in principle, is indivisible as far as the connection between 'objects' and one's own self is concerned. Is there a distinction between the love of oneself and the love of one's neighbour and, if not, what do we mean by selfishness? Self-love is a form of concern or respect for one's own "being" and, as such, it is complementary to that shown to others. To 'love one's neighbour as oneself', implies that respect for the love and understanding of one's own self cannot be separated from the respect, love and understanding for another individual. It seems to me that true self-love is an activity which recognises and values the real, essential self as a function of spiritual "being", in relationship to that of one's fellow man and the "Ground of Being". When Master Eckhart says, *"…if you love all alike, including yourself, you will love them as one person and that person is both God and man.",* is this not an acknowledgement of the reality of shared essence or "being"? A man cannot truly love others if he is unable to love himself. Selfishness, however is a function of the separate 'I' and psychological time, and has nothing to do with the process of love. Consequently, self-love and selfishness, far from being identical, are in fact opposites.

Man, in his normal state of ego-consciousness, perceives a state of separateness which is responsible for his sense of anxiety in different forms. When two people live in a relationship conducted from this perspective, they have not yet learned to love each other. Truly loving relationships experience a sense of connection in the depths of our "being" which is beyond the realm of subject/object duality. This spiritual connection is perceived in the "now" moment but seeks expression in thought, which brings it into the realm of psychological time (which affects the dynamic balance between "being" and "non-being"). When this happens, the relationship becomes subject to the influence of the ego, with its predisposition toward the process of attachment.

Most people's conception of love is the perception of a pleasant sensation. The experience of 'falling in love', when two strangers feel an initial close bond or feeling of oneness, is exciting and all-consuming. The intense feeling of being 'mad' about each other (or infatuation), an illusory indicator of an intensity of love, does not last, because it is a function of the ego and not the essential self.

True love is not just a pleasant sensation but a practical commitment to what is of ultimate concern. Whilst it is a natural consequence of psychological time to form strong attachments and experience deep feelings for those whom we love, many relationships today are based on infatuation, and are primarily a function of ego attachment, where the other person is subconsciously perceived as an object or possession. These may well involve a strong emotional or passionate, physical connection but are not based on a relationship of shared "being". When these relationships are subjected to strain, or the ego attachment weakens, the spiritual commitment to shared "being" is missing, and this is one of the reasons why so many relationships are dysfunctional and eventually break down.

Love is an expression of authentic relatedness at the level of spiritual "being" which is experienced in the "now" moment, beyond the awareness of ego. An act of bravery carried out on the spur of the moment, where a person sacrifices their personal safety or life for the sake of another, is an expression of love, far beyond thought and ego, and is inspired by the 'courage to be'. How often do we hear brave people state that, had they first thought about the situation before acting, they probably would not have taken the action that they did. Spontaneous action in the cause of love is an authentic response to the order of the universe, an action inspired from beyond the limits of psychological time.

The Ending of Psychological Time

Generally the mind is subject to two sources of influence: the ego-dominated cerebral activity of the brain; and an in-built imperative of the nature of "being" with its formative drive toward order and unity with the" Ground of Being" that we have referred to as the spiritual dimension. Krishnamurti talks of the need to end psychological thought and to respond spontaneously to whatever situation exists in the present moment. He is probably saying that we should respond intuitively through action which is prompted from the depths of our "being". This is action, not the result of psychological deliberation or thought, but that which comes about through a spontaneous interaction between soul/particular mind/creative intelligence.

It is my belief that love is the hallmark of authentic intuition which can lead to direct action. This might explain why a person is inspired to take spontaneous action detrimental or harmful to their personal safety, and which would otherwise be inhibited by the process of direct thought. We should develop a heartfelt sensitivity toward a 'fifth dimension' that lies in the depth of our "being" and intuitively guides us toward unity with our fellow man.

Krishnamurti and Bohm[8] point out that love and intelligence are often perceived as personal features, properties or characteristics, instead of as universal phenomena, and a fundamental part of the order of reality. When ego is absent, channels are opened, and the intelligence of universal mind is able to interact with the particular mind through the process of intuitive insight. This facilitates a cognizance of love which, in turn promotes intelligent action, consistent with love.

Is it possible to think about and reflect on our behaviour in a way undefined in terms of psychological time? Any purposeful reflection must involve meditative silence, when the "still small voice" of the soul can be heard intuitively. If we dare to reflect on aspects of our behaviour, the insight gained from intuition can help us to live more intelligently according to the dictates of our soul (heart) in contrast to our brain. The way to reduce the influence of psychological time is to foster an approach to living to heighten our conscious awareness. We must learn to resist the urge to constantly reflect on issues from the 'I' perspective if we are to live in a more authentic manner.

The solution to ending psychological time sounds simple in theory, but the influence of "non-being", in the form of ego, lurks in the shadows waiting to sabotage the whole process, and it is easily activated by the presence of other egos. Until people understand the illusion of psychological time they will be trapped by its influence, and those who understand it will need to maintain a constant state of vigilant awareness to ensure that they do not get sucked into its trap, like water in a whirlpool. If the empty mind is unable to resist the attempts of the ego to break into its silent abode, then love will disappear out of the window and intelligence will go with it.

Do we sometimes confuse cleverness with intelligence? The dictionary implies that cleverness and intelligence are synonymous, but is this true? A person can be clever and have a quick, sharp brain, able to manipulate information and situations, but not all clever people are wise. Intelligence has probably more in common with wisdom and love than with cleverness. This would be consistent with the apprehension of intelligence and wisdom as functions of universal mind and heart-felt action. Cleverness may be perceived as brain-dominated activity, subject to the influence of the ego.

The person who is in touch with the intelligence of the universe, who recognises the presence of their ego and tries hard to eliminate its toxic influence, is aware of a dimension to their lives which is grounded in a reality that they share with others. They intuitively understand the need to promote unity (love) in their relationships with others, and act in ways that seek to unite rather than divide. When they encounter egotistic hostility, they quietly state the truth as they see it and do not allow their ego to get drawn into ill-tempered arguments. They seek to promote the cause of love wherever it may lead and, in so doing, are able to engage with the creative intelligence of universal mind, the source of all wisdom.

Krishnamurti[9] says,

"If love is common to all of us, why am I blind to it?"

The answer appears to be obvious and lies in the fact that to truly love we must first crucify the illusory self or ego. When we come to the realisation that we participate in the process of shared "being" we become aware of the meaning of love and are no longer blind to its recognition, although we may lose sight of it from time to time.

Unless we are a saint, most of us will hover or oscillate between moments of enlightenment, when we shall be free of psychological time, and moments of distraction when it will entangle us in its web. However, I believe that with experience, we learn to recognise its looming shadows and become more skilful in extricating ourselves from its effects.

Summary of Key Ideas

- Psychological time comes into operation when a person is conscious of himself as a separate entity.
- The particular mind can be rational when it operates beyond the influence of psychological time and

irrational when it operates from the perspective of the separate 'I'.
- Man lives in harmony with the universe when his consciousness is conscious of itself or when he acts from a perspective of soul awareness. Disharmony occurs when man's consciousness has given itself an image (ego) which, in reality does not exist.
- The dynamic tension between "being" and "non-being" is the tension between a genetically-inspired struggle for physical survival, conducted by the brain, juxtaposed with a spiritual recognition of the shared essence of "being".
- Love is a general orientation of relatedness of a person to the world as a whole. It is present when people communicate with each other from the centre or essence of their existence, from the perspective of their essential self which transcends the ego.
- Love and intelligence can be viewed as phenomena that are a fundamental part of the order of reality and, as such, are grounded in "Being-itself" and universal mind.
- Intelligence has more in common with wisdom than with cleverness. They are functions of universal mind which are manifested through heart-felt action. Cleverness may be perceived as brain-dominated activity which is subject to the influence of the ego.
- The way to reduce the influence of psychological time is to foster an approach to living which heightens our conscious awareness of "being".

CHAPTER 4.

The Nature of Faith

Faith as Ultimate Concern

Paul Tillich[1] defines faith as the state of being ultimately concerned. He points out that man has many concerns (e.g. food and shelter) some of which are urgent. The concern which claims ultimacy demands the total commitment of him who accepts this claim. One could say that such an ultimate concern is a person's god.

Idolatrous Faith

Tillich maintains that if faith is the state of being ultimately concerned, everybody would appear to have a faith of some description, which has a specific content, because everybody has a concern which they perceive to be ultimate. If your ultimate concern is your country then the content of your faith will be patriotic concern for its best interests above all others. People whose ultimate concern is money will be absorbed with generating wealth, and those who crave success or stardom will be focused on 'climbing the ladder' or becoming a celebrity.

However, what if the content of this faith and its associated god proves to be illusory and is shown to be less than ultimate? The concern may have appeared to the individual to have been totally unconditional and ultimate but eventually it is shown to be inauthentic. If this happens the meaning of one's life breaks down, the faith and its associated god disappears leaving a void at the centre of the 'believer', what Viktor Frankl would call an existential vacuum. The nature of the faith is revealed as idolatrous, as less than ultimate and, unless it is replaced by a new content of ultimate concern, the individual is liable to feel the despair of a meaningless existence.

We see many examples in life where people discover that their personal god is less than ultimate, and experience the sense of disillusionment and suffering that accompanies this realisation. When Hitler came to power in Germany during the 1930s he had a personal aura which was holy in a demonic way. Many saw him as a great leader who would restore pride and respect to the German people following the humiliation of the First World War. Their ultimate concern, or faith, became the Fatherland and they regarded Hitler as a god-like figure who would lead them to great things in the future. Millions of men were so passionate about their faith that they were prepared to fight bravely and die for their country.

However, many were unable or unwilling to see Hitler as a megalomaniac and were deluded by the propaganda fed to them through the media. Many of his followers were also influenced by the power of his rhetoric and lost the ability to use their own discriminatory powers of reason to question what was happening. This is particularly true of those who perpetrated hideous crimes in the concentration camps, whilst they showed care and concern toward their own families. By the time many realised the idolatrous nature of their faith, a lot of the damage had been done and they were powerless to change the status quo, or turn back the clock.

Other examples can be seen in everyday life where, for example, those who make money their god can sometimes fall prey to corruption. Others devote their lives to making money and neglect their children, as they are unable to spend enough quality time with them and give them the love and attention they need to grow into loving, balanced adults. They rationalise their preoccupation with money by convincing themselves that they are providing for the material needs of the family. They believe that they are giving their children a good start in life, providing a good standard of living and some are mystified when their children go "off the rails". People who become ultimately concerned with their physical appearance and are obsessed with how they look will, sooner or later, experience the transitory nature of their god as the ageing process eventually takes its toll.

We can see that those who become ultimately concerned with physical appearance, celebrity, materialism or jingoism are likely to experience the illusory nature of these concerns. If this happens the meaning of one's life breaks down, one's personal centre has been given away and the idolatrous nature of the faith is revealed. Is it not significant that all forms of idolatrous faith have their origin in the ego which is itself an illusory creation of the mind?

Does this mean then that we cannot enjoy the benefits of living in an industrial society? Must we forgo the pleasures of good food, cultural entertainment and leisure, and the developments of new technology? Is it wrong to take a pride in our appearance or wear attractive clothes and do we have to be serious and frightened to enjoy ourselves? We have said that man has many concerns and there is no reason why he should not enjoy the material pleasures of this world. What is significant is the level of importance that he attaches to his material existence, and the problem arises when he attaches ultimate importance to something that is less than ultimate.

Ultimate concern as a Function of Timeless Reality (Beyond Psychological Time)

When we think about life we realise that the human body is a hive of activity with millions of different cells working together for the good of the organism. There seems to be a vital energy, or process operating that arises from our "being". This must surely have a source that is rooted in unmanifest reality, a phenomenon to which Tillich refers as "Being-itself". Could it be that it is this reality, a flowing process, to which we are referring when we use the word 'God'? Could it be that this is the fount of energy that gives rise to the flux of life that dwells within all living creatures, a phenomenon that is neither subject nor object, both immanent and transcendent? Furthermore, if this is the case, we are talking about a flowing process of energy that is active, a verb not a noun, which makes the subject/object distinction between God and man inappropriate. I believe that this makes the theistic view of God difficult to rationalise and part of the reason why it is difficult to define faith in terms of concrete content.

Although man's experiences, feelings and thoughts are conditioned and finite, he is driven towards faith by an awareness of the infinite to which he feels a sense of connection, a reality which is part of his identity and transcends it. If man is to have an ultimate concern, it must be related to the "Ground of Being", and must reasonably embrace the relationship of his own "being" with that of his fellow man. It is this realisation that provides man with a true sense of identity, not the illusory ego which distracts and confuses the issue through the process of psychological time.

If we accept that man's ultimate concern must be to pursue a way of life which leads to unity between his "being" and what Tillich calls the "Ground of Being" or "Being-itself", this implies the pursuit of unity between his "being" and that of his fellow man, because they are inextricably linked. Any other concern will be less than ultimate, ego-linked, and although it may have an unconditional hold over the individual that appears to be ultimate, the faith it inspires is destined to be idolatrous.

If man's ultimate concern is not a function of the ego and is of a spiritual nature, it must seek expression outside psychological time or in the eternal "now" moment. What form will this expression take, because we are trying to express a timeless reality in terms of temporal activity? How are we to define the qualities or values which will give concrete expression to this ultimate concern or faith?

The Nature of the Spiritual and the Psychophysical

The eminent psychiatrist Viktor Frankl, who survived the horrors of the concentration camps at Auschwitz and Dachau, believed that the unconscious was not simply driven by instincts. Unlike Freud, who saw only unconscious instinct, it was Frankl's belief that the unconscious may be divided into what he called unconscious instinctuality and unconscious spirituality. He suggested that the dichotomy between conscious and unconscious was a secondary issue and that the essential problem was one of spiritual existence versus, what he referred to as, psychophysical facticity. I presume that his use of the word 'facticity' referred to the Heideggerian term which means the sum total of our current situation and all our future possibilities which are the consequence of being thrust into an existence not of our choice.

The essence of our existence is spiritual energy that we call "being", but this existence is lived within the physical world of form and within the context of time and space. Our life is given form in terms of the physiology of our body and the psychology of our mind. The purpose of life, I believe, is to integrate these different aspects of existence in a way that is in tune with the order of the universe and leads to a sense of holism and inner harmony. And the kernel of meaning in life, the focus of that which is of ultimate concern, is embryonic within the spiritual dimension of our "being", and seeks expression in the world of form through the psychological and physiological aspects of existence (what we call psychophysical activity).

If the origin of meaning lies within the essence of our "being", what is its nature? It is energy-related and linked to the energy of the universe which is creative and intelligent. If the energy of our "being" is grounded in a sea of energy that gives form to reality and the universe, the two must be connected. It would seem reasonable to suggest that all life experiences connectivity with this sea of energy (what we have referred to as the universal flux or "Ground of Being") and that all human beings will experience a specific form of connection. I conceive that the energy of our "being", in its natural state, interacts synchronously with the "Ground of Being". Furthermore, there is the same potential for synchronistic interaction between human beings where the energy of their "being" resonates harmoniously. This natural state in which we are conscious of a synchronistic, resonant interaction of our "being" with the "Ground of Being" and with the "being" of our fellow man, is what we call soul awareness, and the synchronicity we experience is what we call love, which manifests itself as joy and a sense of peace

This is a spiritual reality which we experience ontologically within the depths of our "being", and is the source of meaningful relationships. Authentic living is concerned with making this spiritual reality explicit, within the context of time and space, through psychophysical activity. It is my belief that ontological meaning resides in spirit and that the purpose of life is to translate this into ontic meaning in the world of form, through psychophysical activity which manifests this reality.

However, the pursuit of authentic living is not straightforward because our conscious concern with everyday events draws us away from consciousness of the spiritual dimension. Consequently, life can be lived inauthentically from the perspective of subject /object duality, that brings into play the activity of the ego. When this happens a sense of fragmentation occurs to disrupt the sense of holism between the spiritual and the psychophysical (or if you like, between body, mind and soul). This may be sensed as feelings of disquiet, meaninglessness or guilt, the magnitude of which will be related to the degree or strength of ego involvement.

Some individuals are completely insensitive to the spiritual dimension and capable of perpetrating hideous acts of cruelty best described as evil. Their sense of meaning is not derived from their spiritual centre but arises purely from a psychophysical view of reality corrupted by dualistic perceptions. Consequently their brain fails to take cognizance of shared humanity, responds to the misperceptions of its illusory self and indulges in irrational, driven behaviour fuelled by emotion which can be cruel, vindictive and pathological.

How do we translate the imperative to love into meaningful psychophysical activity if love is a spiritual reality which fades from view when we turn to conscious thought that can be influenced by psychological time? It is impossible to define love, which can only be experienced in the "now" moment, but is there a way in which love can manifest itself as a meaning, and not be the product of conscious thought? I believe that this is possible through the process that we call intuition. This is the product of unconscious spiritual activity (energy) which communicates with the psychophysical through feeling and thought that arises unconsciously and is not the product of direct brain-related thought.

How could this happen? The reader may recall that, in Chapter 2, we showed that man's knowledge is not absolute and is based on models or art forms which attempt to explain his perceptions. In view of what contemporary science is suggesting about the nature of reality, and the models or art forms it uses to depict this reality, it would appear conceivable that man's form is the product of a complex arrangement of interacting energy fields. These may well relate to specific centres within the body that are capable of interacting with the universal flux.

Could it be that when the individual is in a state of soul awareness, the energy fields which relate to his form may be able to interact with the universal flux, in a way that facilitates energy exchange manifested in thought and feelings? If such a process was possible it may enable the individual to access a form of intelligence to guide his behaviour, leading to wise action. Could this be what the Buddhists refer to as a state of 'mindfulness' which gives direction to psychophysical activity?

Faith and Reason

Is faith rational or are reason and faith mutually exclusive? If faith is understood as the state of being ultimately concerned, then Tillich feels that no conflict exists, and I agree. We must first ask ourselves what the word reason means in the context of faith. Firstly we need to bear in mind what we have said about knowledge: it is not absolute; it is based on our limited perception of reality; is structured in the form of conceptual frameworks or patterns which are stored in the mind; and these are the outcome of thoughts which are a 'dance of the mind'. It is clear that man has no absolute knowledge of reality and is only able to develop theories or models which resonate with his perceptions. Reason is the cognitive facility that provides a meaningful structure to review man's use of concepts to explain his perceptions of reality, in a way which has some measure of inner consistency or 'ring of truth'. If faith is to be rational it must resonate with man's perception of reality in a way which appeals to reason.

If faith is the state of being ultimately concerned, and one's concern is truly ultimate, there should be no conflict between faith and reason. If our ultimate concern is a quest for unity between personal "being" and "Being-itself", and this is indeed ultimate, the individual should experience a feeling of peace and harmony, a manifestation of the resonance of his "being" with the essence of reality. Furthermore, reason suggests that the individual will recognise the nature of his shared "being" and consequently seek to find unity and peace with his fellow man. The conscious awareness of this principle seems reasonable and self-evident, so why is this ultimate concern, this "faith", distorted under the conditions of human existence?

Tillich would say that it is affected by the presence of "non-being" within man's "being". We discussed this earlier and suggested that it was related to man's loss of awareness of his true identity as "being" and his pre-occupation with his illusory self. It is the ego which causes the distortion within faith and reason, and it does this by causing separation between the individual, his fellow man and the "Ground of Being". When this happens, he feels a sense of estrangement which destroys his sense of peace and unity, because he loses touch with the timeless dimension of his soul and becomes entangled in psychological time.

Man's problem is that he has to live in the world of time and space. He has to give order to what we have called psychophysical activity and to do this he has to make use of his brain to think. His faith, his ultimate concern for unity is a timeless, spiritual imperative which is of the soul, and man, in his everyday living has to find a way of life which resonates with what is his true, spiritual, essential nature. He has to create a cognitive framework to complement the spiritual dimension if he is to avoid a feeling of estrangement. However, man's susceptibility to psychological time promotes the ego and fragmented thought which is irrational, destroys reason and undermines faith.

How should we seek to overcome the problem of estrangement? Clearly, we have to examine our own behaviour intuitively to see that it promotes a sense of unity in our dealings with each other. We must remain attentive and seek to maintain a high level of conscious awareness of our behaviour and how it relates to our true nature.

You may say, quite legitimately, that it is difficult to promote unity in our dealings with others when they are aggressive, self-centred and seeking to exploit us. I would understand that point of view but would suggest that the quest for unity will not be easy and does not imply that we allow others to dominate and exploit us. It does not mean that we stand aside and allow misguided people to manipulate and bully those who seek unity, peace and harmony. We have to stand firm and express the truth of reality as we intuitively perceive it to be and challenge the behaviour of those who seek to be divisive. This may require great courage and sacrifice but we must endeavour to follow this course in a way which tries to avoid judgementalism.

We have to recognise that those who would be our adversaries are acting from a position which lacks conscious awareness of their true essence. Somehow we must never forget that to take offense, hold a grudge and to seek revenge is the process of psychological time, that it leads to a disturbance of the dynamic between "being" and "non-being" and cuts off the individual from the power of "Being-itself". Whoever pursues that route will only promote "non-being" that will lead to further conflict and suffering.

We have emphasised the fact that our theories and insights concerning reality are not fixed and our conceptual structures are evolving and adapting to new experience. One has only to look at the state of the world to see that there is great scope for radical change in the future. The reality of everyday living is such that the vast majority of people do not live their lives from the perspective of what is of ultimate concern, or have any concept of what this means. There is a need to raise awareness of faith as of ultimate concern and what this entails in terms of the values which influence our behaviour.

Putting this another way, man will continually need to reflect on whether the way he lives is consistent with his ultimate concern and, when problems arise, he will need to use his powers of reason and intuition to resolve them. This will be an evolutionary process, continually leading to new insights that result in a change to what is seen as an authentic element in the psychophysical content that gives expression to his ultimate concern. Wherever such revelatory experience occurs, both faith and reason are renewed, their internal and mutual conflicts are resolved (at least temporarily), and a feeling of estrangement is replaced by reconciliation. Given the nature of reality, the psychophysical realisation of love (as ultimate concern) requires a response which is appropriate to the psychophysical reality which presents itself in the "now" moment.

In principle, there appears to be no conflict between faith

and reason and if we are to make religious faith credible in the twenty-first century, then it is necessary to show that it can be related to other forms of cognitive reason. Harris was dismissive of faith which bore no relationship to other forms of knowledge, but the reader may recall that his argument was not directed at Tillich who tried to address this issue.

All forms of knowledge try to express truth in the sense of what Tillich calls the "really real". He appears to be saying that man is trying to reach truth in the sense of what "rings true" both within the cognitive function of the human mind and in the depths of the soul (he is searching for wholeness and authenticity). Faith as an ultimate concern seeks to express the spiritual imperative of love in psychophysical terms for everyday living. It cannot be separated from everyday affairs and therefore must relate to other forms of knowledge and reason. If not it has no practical value.

Different forms of knowledge are based on conceptual frameworks that attempt to model the reality perceived within the universe. Tillich[2] says the truth of faith is different from the meaning of truth in other forms of knowledge. What could he mean? I believe he was referring to the way in which 'truth' is perceived in these different branches of knowledge. Where 'spiritual truth' differs to 'scientific truth' is in the way their particular conceptions of truth are perceived. 'Religious/spiritual truth' also has implications for the way life is lived.

The Truth of Faith and Scientific Truth

Science tries to describe and to explain the structures and relations in the universe, in so far as they can be tested by experiment and calculated in quantitative terms. It makes use of data and information obtained through the senses (e.g. visual observation) and organises these perceptions into concepts and theories. The truth of a scientific statement is the adequacy of its description of the structural laws as they relate to reality. Every 'scientific truth' is subject to changes, both in grasping reality, and in expressing it adequately, but the fact that it is not absolute does not diminish its 'truth value' in explaining the outcome of experimental observation. The history of science is a history of scientific revolutions where theories that were held to be firmly established (e.g. Ptolemy's Cosmology, Dalton's Atomic Theory) had to be discarded because they could not explain the facts of subsequent experimental observation. The fact is that a scientific statement is only based on a model which is used to explain what is observed in the real world, or what is deemed to be "really real" by the cognitive function of the human mind. It tries to explain and predict reality, it is not absolute truth.

There is a parallel between the development of scientific knowledge and religious experience. Scientific knowledge grew from observation of the physical world and reflection on those observations. For thousands of years man has stood in awe and wonder of the miracle of creation and has sought ways to explain many of life's mysteries. It is not difficult to see why early man came to worship the sun as a powerful reality or god which provided him with warmth and food to eat. It is no surprise that when thunderstorms and earthquakes occurred, or volcanoes erupted that he felt that the gods were angry. Man was trying to make sense of his world, something he has been doing ever since those early times. He was puzzled and afraid of those things which he did not understand and, in his insecurity, sought explanations which could provide him with peace of mind.

As time passed, he developed an awareness of a reality which he felt to be a part of his inner "being" and yet much greater than himself. He conceived that this reality, which he called God, was his creator, the source and sustainer of his life who provided for his needs. Man's experience of family life provided a conceptual framework which he used to try and comprehend a reality which he sensed but could not see. Man perceived that he was created in God's image and so he came to view God as a heavenly father, a provider who behaved in the same way as he did with his own family. Conceptually he visualised this God as a being who lived in another realm above the skies, but religious concepts, like scientific concepts need to change and evolve when they do not resonate with reality. Space travel has shown this concept to be inappropriate and I doubt if any serious theologian would think of God in this way. However, religion has been slow to respond to changing perceptions of reality and consequently, many people believe that it is irrelevant to modern living.

We can see that that both religion and science are different ways in which man has attempted to understand reality, they are attempts to grasp what is "really real", what "rings true" with the cognitive function of the human mind. However, they are fundamentally different in the way they perceive reality. Physical Science is concerned with the understanding of manifest reality, which is accessible to the five senses and has a physical referent. Religion, on the other hand, is concerned with understanding the nature of unmanifest reality which is invisible, has no physical referent but can be accessed through intuition. I believe that it is the lack of a physical referent which has made it difficult to communicate the reality of religious faith and led to a preoccupation with dogmatic belief.

During the course of history, certain individuals, who possessed a heightened spiritual awareness, were born in different cultural settings. They tried to convey their insights to their contemporaries but, because of the difficulty involved in the communication of spiritual reality in the form of language, I believe that their messages were not always understood and the use of parables, myths and literal information, to convey 'spiritual truth', became confused and dogmatic. In recent centuries, with the evolution of man's understanding of the nature of knowledge and reason, religion has come under the spotlight and many aspects of its dogma have been questioned, and quite rightly so. Whilst science has progressed quickly, especially in the field of electronics, spiritual awareness has disintegrated to such an extent that there is an alarming increase in the degree of disillusionment and the sense of meaninglessness felt within society. Families split up under the pressure created by a materialistic society which has lost its spiritual centre. How has this happened?

Man feels that he has all the answers, that he is the master of his ship and that his science can explain everything, but this is not the case. Could it be that his ship is rudderless? Has he lost his bearings? Will he get to the right destination? Science makes use of the physical senses to support its brand of truth, but is there another dimension which we can access that puts us in touch with who we really are, which acts like a compass and gives us a true sense of direction so that we do not get lost on the ocean of life? I believe that the spiritual dimension provides this sense of direction, so why have the majority turned away from it?

The answer is that they cannot relate to the dogmatic messages which are offered by some of the religious faiths in the twenty-first century. Religious thinking has not evolved in the same way as science and modern man does not relate to concepts that do not 'ring true' with his perception of reality. Some people within the Christian community have written on this subject and see no future for organised religion unless there is a radical change in the way it is presented (e.g. John Shelby Spong). How can we change the status quo?

It seems to me that religious faith, as ultimate concern, and science have something in common, in so far as they can both make use of the power of reason to question the integrity or validity of the models they use to express their truth. Faith, as ultimate concern, is necessary to provide man with a conception of his real self as "being", and to give his life a sense of meaning and direction.

The Truth of Faith and Historical Truth

Tillich[3] says that the truth of faith cannot be made dependant on the historical truth of the stories and legends in which faith has expressed itself. It is a disastrous distortion of the meaning of faith to identify it with the belief in the historical validity of the Biblical stories. The 'truth of the faith' will depend on how well its psychophysical expression manifests what is of ultimate concern, how it rings true, how it expresses what is spiritually "really real" to the individual believer. I believe that religion places too much emphasis on historical figures and on defending the validity of historical information, recorded in documents shrouded in the past. What matters is not whether the facts in the Bible or Koran are historically true but whether the messages they convey ring true in the depths of our soul and, in my opinion, are consistent with love.

Surely faith, as an ultimate concern, should seek to focus on some of the values which have sought expression in different cultural settings. When Jesus talked about the parable of the "Good Samaritan" and the Buddha talked about the importance of compassion, were they not both talking about the same thing? It is time for people of different faiths to leave the past behind, to focus on love as their ultimate concern and how this spiritual reality can be made manifest within the psychophysical realm of form in time and space. They could then speak with one voice, inspire and provide guidance to the majority who are searching for spiritual direction and meaning.

Given the nature of reality as a flowing process, we should anticipate the inevitability of fresh, new insights in the development of the psychophysical manifestation of the spiritual with the evolution of mankind. It's not dogma that is important but whether the substance of what is said leads to the pursuit of what is of ultimate concern. Now is the time to remove the cancer of dogmatic fundamentalism (whether this be of Christian, Jewish or Muslim origin), a malfunction rooted within the framework of fragmentary thought and shrouded in history.

The Truth of Faith and Philosophical Truth

Tillich[4] says,

"The difficulty of every discussion concerning philosophy as such is the fact that every definition of philosophy is an expression of the point of view of the philosopher who gives the definition."

He defines philosophy as the attempt to answer the most general questions about the nature of reality and human existence. It would appear that it could be described, in principle, as a detached description of how reality appears to manifest itself. The philosophy of faith is therefore a description of that which appears to be of ultimate concern. Broadly, this is tantamount to saying that it is the psychophysical expression which aims to give ultimate meaning to the way that life is lived.

Faith accepts the validity of this expression of what is of ultimate concern and makes a commitment to live accordingly. Religious faith is, therefore, the commitment by an individual to actualising his philosophical, psychophysical vision within the context of the reality of everyday life. This suggests that it is the role of the philosophy of faith to give direction to man's psychophysical response to the spiritual reality of love which is of ultimate concern. Faith is then a commitment to live in accordance with a philosophical vision seen as resonant with reality.

When we talk about what is of ultimate concern we are talking about life itself, or that which is its essence. This is the unknown which cannot be observed with the five senses and can only be grasped by intuitive insight. This is a subjective process, focused on intuitive feelings which seek expression in terms of thought and concepts. The philosophy of faith is therefore a subjective attempt to capture or express, in concepts, the essence or the nature of spirit which gives form to life. It is not an expression of reality as it is but an attempt to give an indication or pointer to its nature, through an intuitive feeling for what is of value. The truth of the philosophy of faith is therefore related to how well its concepts or values describe the intuitive perceptions we have about the nature or essence of spirit. When we talk about issues of ultimate concern we are talking about values, measurements concerning the immeasurable. It would appear that the truth of our philosophy of faith is linked to how well its measured values coincide with the immeasurable. This sounds paradoxical so how do we know and how can we make an assessment? There is no objective test! This would imply that all attempts to define faith in psychophysical terms are subjective and limited.

What does Tillich mean when he talks about the truth of faith? He says that it can only be expressed in symbols, implying an acknowledgement of the limitations of language in expressing spiritual reality which occurs in the moment. I believe that the truth of faith reveals itself through the heartfelt conviction in the authenticity of what is of ultimate concern and the soul's commitment to live according to that concern. The truth of faith is that which rings true in the depths of one's "being", it is related to the conviction we show in the pursuit of that faith, and it manifests itself through the courage to be our essential self.

However, we have alluded to the fact that our perceptions of reality will change in response to changes in our perceptual awareness. When this happens intuitive insight may alert the individual to the fact that there is incongruity between the way he lives and the cognitive structures which give substance to the philosophy of his faith. This would suggest that either, he needs to review his psychophysical response to faith (i.e. that changing perceptions of reality reveal a need for him to adapt his thoughts and behaviour to new situations) or, that his commitment to that faith is less than absolute (i.e. that something is affecting the commitment of his heart and soul to the philosophical vision).

The dissonance experienced will be resolved either, by making conceptual changes to the framework which underpins his philosophy and acting on this, or by identifying and removing the barrier undermining his commitment to faith. In the case of the latter, the cause is likely to have its root within the realm of psychological time. There is a need for mind and soul to work in tandem if the individual is to find true peace of mind and for this to happen, there must be a synchronicity between the philosophical truth and the practice of faith. We have already discussed in depth the insidious nature of psychological time and the importance of intuitive insight in matters of faith. It is when heart and mind work together that we become more adept at recognising the presence of "non-being" and we learn to live more authentically.

When you consider what we have said in the previous paragraphs you begin to understand the paradoxical nature of faith and the difficulty of trying to express ultimate concern in psychophysical terms. Psychophysical expression is evolutionary and adapts to our changing perceptions of reality. It is unable to express in word and thought the essence of love, a timeless spiritual phenomenon that is experienced in the "now" moment. It seems the psychophysical expression of love cannot be expressed in language but only through action prompted through spontaneous heart-felt intuition (actions speak louder than words).

The Christian faith may have been in decline for the past two hundred years or more because the philosophical truth of traditional Christianity does not coincide completely with our perception of reality in the twenty-first century. Many Christians are conscious of some aspects that do not match their perceptions, concepts like the virgin birth that do not appear possible in reality. Why is it the case so many Christians today are committed to the truth of their faith, seeing it as consistent with some aspect of reality which resonates deep within their soul whilst, at the same time, they have deep reservations about much of the dogma they are expected to believe?

We suggested earlier that religious faith is related to the commitment of the essential self to actualising its philosophical vision, psychophysically within the context of the reality of everyday life. If this is the case why are many Christians able to practise a faith when they are not completely convinced of the philosophical truth of that faith? It is my conviction that it is the commitment to love which is the essential element within the truth of faith and that it is the actualising of the precept of Jesus, to love one's neighbour as oneself, which is the essential, significant, over-riding element of the truth of the philosophy of Christian faith. Any person who lives their life in accordance with these commitments is living in a way which synchronises with the spiritual reality of the universe. I believe that much of Christian dogma is superfluous, but it is the commitment to love which rings true in the depths of the soul. It is my view that this is probably the main reason why the Christian faith has survived for two thousand years and why many people, like John Shelby Spong, are unwilling to completely let it go.

Tillich says that there is philosophical truth in the truth of faith. If we view faith as a commitment to our ultimate concern of shared "being" (love), then the philosophical truth of this faith is that enlightenment, or salvation, is achieved through the death of the illusory self (ego) which results in a union of man's spiritual "being" with the source of its creation and with that of his fellow man.

It appears to me to be ironic that we are talking about a form of sacrifice and that both Judaism and Christianity have laid great emphasis on the importance of this practice. In the case of Judaism this took the form of animal sacrifice, whereas Christianity regarded the death of Jesus as a sacrifice of God's son to God himself. Our perception of reality today recognises the role of the ego in human suffering and relates to the need for the crucifixion of this illusory form of self in order for the essential self to live authentically and reveal its true "being". I believe that the symbol of the Cross, in this context is much more meaningful today.

Faith and Love

The consciousness of ultimate identity with the "Ground of Being" is what makes identification with all beings necessary. Faith, as the act of being ultimately concerned implies love, namely: the desire and urge toward the reunion of the separated. Tillich[5] says,

"Can a man love who has no ultimate concern?...The answer,

of course, is that there is no human being without an ultimate concern and, in this sense without faith. Love is present, even if hidden, in a human being; for every human being is longing for union with the content of his ultimate concern."

This is interesting because Tillich seems to imply that all human beings have the same ultimate concern at the centre of their "being"; that, deep down, they are all searching to be reunited with the "Ground of Being". The problem is that they do not recognise what they are searching for and their true ultimate concern becomes masked psychophysically by the effects of the ego. I am sure that there are times when everybody experiences moments when they feel a real rapport with another human being. This often happens when somebody acts in an unselfish way to do something to enhance the well-being of another. Unselfish acts come from the heart and are a function of the essential-self, acting beyond the influence of the ego or false self.

At moments like these there is a bonding between the two individuals, no barrier exists between them and their mutual concern is as one. When this happens there is an experience of non-separation, or love, which springs from the core of their "being" and resonates or harmonises with the "Ground of Being". This experience is often accompanied by a feeling of joy. Unfortunately, each of us has an ego which exerts a very strong influence and can take control over the way we behave unless we are conscious of the way it works. When Tillich says that love is present, even hidden in a human being, he is really saying that the ego of that person is the dominant influence and masking his true "being" or essential self.

Like Tillich, I believe that the rejection of faith today is rooted in a misunderstanding of the nature of faith and this is because faith is a concept, a reality which is difficult to grasp and to describe. If faith is understood as ultimate concern it justifies itself against those who attack it. The problem lies with what many people perceive to be their ultimate concern and whether or not it is rooted in love.

Faith and Courage

Man's predicament is that the human situation is disposed toward estrangement and separation and this is the root cause of so much suffering. Genuine faith expresses the desire to break down barriers and build bridges, to re-unite man with the "Ground of Being" and with his fellow man.

Faith is something which ebbs and flows, sometimes we are so conscious of our ultimate concern, whilst at other times it fades from view in the mist of psychological time. On occasions, we can feel a close relationship with "Being-itself" and our fellow man and at other times we experience a feeling of separation. Just as there is a dynamic relationship between "being" and "non-being", there appears to be a similar dynamic between the certainty of faith and the doubt of faith, which leads to a spectrum of different feelings. Jesus himself experienced this dynamic tension and it seems that man can never be completely certain because he cannot fully eliminate the element of doubt. This cannot be otherwise, if we accept the fact that, all the insights of man are expressed in conceptual structures which are subject to change.

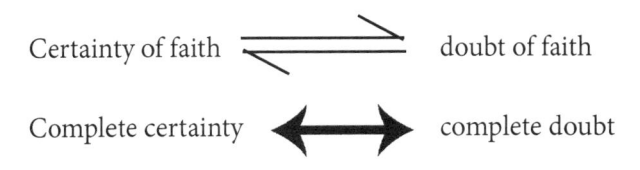

Certainty of faith ⇌ doubt of faith

Complete certainty ⟷ complete doubt

Tillich says that those who rest on their unshakeable faith, described as fanatics, are showing the unmistakeable symptoms of doubt which has been repressed. He says that doubt is not overcome by repression but by courage. Courage does not deny that there is doubt but it takes the doubt into itself as an expression of its own finitude and affirms the content of an ultimate concern. We shall now explore the relationship between faith and the courage to be oneself.

Summary of Key Ideas

- Reality appears to be an active process involving energy. Could it be that it is this flowing process to which we are referring when we use the word 'God'?
- Tillich defines faith as the state of being ultimately concerned. Ultimate concern must be linked to the process of "being" which is grounded in the universal flux of energy.
- Authentic faith is a function of the soul, whereas inauthentic or idolatrous faith is connected with the concerns of the ego, which are less than ultimate.
- Faith, as ultimate concern, must focus on love as the process of shared "being". Loss of awareness of this process within psychological time undermines faith and leads to estrangement.
- Faith as ultimate concern seeks psychophysical expression in everyday living. It cannot be separated from everyday affairs and therefore must relate to other forms of knowledge and reason.
- I believe that the truth of faith is revealed by a heartfelt, intuitive feeling that expresses an authentic

relatedness to the spiritual reality of love. It is that which rings true in the depths of one's "being", it is related to the conviction we show in the pursuit of the faith and it reveals itself in the courage to be one's essential self.
- All human beings have the same ultimate concern at the centre of their "being": that, deep down, they are all searching to be reunited with the "Ground of Being". The problem is that many do not recognise what they are searching for and the ego is the dominant influence in their lives.
- Faith is not absolute but a phenomenon which ebbs and flows. Just as there is a dynamic relationship between "being" and "non-being", there appears to be a similar dynamic between the certainty of faith and the doubt of faith which leads to a spectrum of different feelings.
- Tillich says that those who rest on their unshakeable faith, who are fanatical, are showing the unmistakeable symptoms of doubt which has been repressed. He says that doubt is overcome, not by repression but by courage.

CHAPTER 5.

Faith and The Courage to be Oneself

Many people today pride themselves on knowing who they are as a person but what does this mean? If they are referring to a mental image of whom they believe themselves to be then the chances are that they are deluding themselves, for this will have been conceived psychophysically within the context of psychological time.

Frank Sinatra had a hit single with the song 'My Way', with lyrics appealing to a lot of people. They related to a person who met life head-on, enjoying the good times and facing up to the bad without dwelling on regrets. They identified with someone who had a plan, who knew where he or she was going, who did not deviate from that course and faced up to, and overcame any doubts along the way. They implied that somebody who has the courage to be their own self is to be admired but what is this 'self' we are talking about?

Most of us respect a person who is able to confront trials and difficulties and would view courage as the fortitude which enables a person to face up to anxiety and fear, to pursue a course of action which they feel to be right, in spite of the consequences. Let us look more closely at the concept of 'self' and see if we can make sense of what it means to be oneself. We can then explore what we mean by the courage to be oneself and examine how it relates to anxiety, fear, psychological time and faith.

What is a self?

Julian Baggini, in his book 'The Ego Trick', is intrigued by the fact that, during the course of time, we seem to change completely and yet paradoxically remain the same. He suggests[1] that most people experience a sense of 'me-ness', an essence or core of self that holds steady through life. He refers to this as the 'pearl view' but acknowledges a problem with this conception of reality, in so far as nobody is able to locate this 'precious gem'. We discussed this briefly in Chapter 1 when we suggested that we can never discover the experiencer of an experience. If this enduring essence is that which makes somebody the same person throughout their life he wants to know what and where it is.

Maybe, the problem lies in the fact that man has to live in the world of time and space and in order to do this he has to adopt some form of identity. Practical living requires an individual identity, but man's essence is his sense of "being" which is a process grounded in the universal flux. A crude analogy can be drawn with a wave on the ocean, in so far as the wave has an individual form which is recognisable but its real essence is the continuous body of water which constitutes the ocean.

If man wishes to live in a way which is authentic and acknowledges his essence as "being", he needs to live as an individual who recognises that this essence is not of an individual nature, that his true nature is not an entity but the process of "being". This is paradoxical because it is not semantically possible to be both an entity and a process at the same time. I believe that Galen Strawson recognises this problem (to which Baggini makes reference[2]) when he makes the statement that self-experience exists, as a form of experience, whether or not selves do.

Man has to live in time and space in a way which integrates the sensual illusion of his individuality with the reality of his essence as "being". He appears to have two frames of reference which are related to whether, or not, his consciousness is trapped within psychological time. Is it possible to define the word 'self' in a way which recognises our essence as "being", that acknowledges that there is no personal subject that we call 'I' but at the same time acknowledges our separate form. Perhaps this is possible if we view our existence in terms of a 'selfless self' that recognises the existence of a consciousness that experiences, but not from the perspective of a subjective 'I' (see Figure 1.1, Diagram (b), p. 7). The selfless self (what I have previously referred to as the 'essential self') tries to interpret this experience from a perspective of shared "being" and not from the perspective of a personal ego. When man is able to live from this perspective, he aligns himself with the order of the universe and experiences a synchronicity with the universal flux. He knows intuitively that the acknowledgement of shared "being" or love is an authentic way to live and experiences a sense of peace and inner harmony. This process is sabotaged by the brain's propensity toward psychological time which leads to a dislocation from his perception of shared "being". When he lives from this perspective he loses a sense of inner peace and harmony, he lives in the changeable world of the separate 'I' and can lose his sense of integrity and authenticity. So what is this selfless self?

If man lives from the perception of himself as a separate 'I', with no awareness of his essence as "being", he will be egotistic and snapshots of his personality, taken at different times, will reflect a variety of different personae. If he recognises that his essence is "being" and he is able to live within the context of time and space with this realisation at the forefront of his mind, he will have no fixed self-image or ego and will live from the perspective of love as an ultimate concern which drives his personality. He will view himself as a process in contrast to an entity and flow with the changing conditions of life, attempting to live in the moment. He who is conscious of "being" flows with the different experiences of life and does not identify with them from the perspective of a separate 'I' (i.e. he is selfless in so far as he has eliminated the ego, or separate 'I').

The states of consciousness to which we have referred as the 'selfless self', or the separate 'I', are two polarised modes of existence which relate to the abstract terms of "being" and "non-being". Our perception of self is never constant and varies across a spectrum defined in terms of abstract extremes, characterised by complete selflessness and extreme egotism. Most of us live in a way that is egotistic to some degree because we live in the world of time and space, with its emphasis on sensory perception and thought.

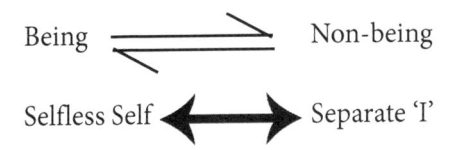

Being ⇌ Non-being

Selfless Self ⟷ Separate 'I'

Our human organism exists in time and space, in the form

of a body with a heart, brain and mind, all working together to create an interpretation of reality. This is done by using our different senses to gather perceptions which are translated into pictures, sounds, feelings, smells, tastes and thoughts. These contribute toward the collection of vast amounts of information, probably in the form of different configurations of energy, which are processed, organised and stored in some way as units of experience etc.

These units (that comprise a vast range of cognitive structures, feelings, physiological characteristics etc.) interact in a multitude of ways and contribute psychophysically toward a sense of self, a personality that gives us the impression that we are a unitary entity. Our brain is aware of different combinations of units (configurations of energy) that come into consciousness in response to certain stimuli and create the impression of a self and behaviour that can change according to different circumstances. Sometimes we can feel full of confidence, whilst at other times we lack belief in our abilities. Our awareness of different units of experience can change momentarily leading to different thoughts and feelings. Furthermore, these units evolve in response to new experiences and our physiology changes with time, leading to the perception of a self and body that changes.

We have an enduring conviction that we have a central core or self, but when we try to define this entity we are unable to do so. This is because the brain is trying to pin something down, i.e. our personality, which is continually moving and changing. We are unable to discover a stable, unchanging self as personality because the units which comprise our perception of this phenomenon change with experience, and what we see as our self is in a constant state of flux. The perceived changing self is the ever-changing, psychophysical, physiological, mind/brain generated conception which is created within time.

Baggini is opposed to the idea of a self as unchanging immortal essence. I would argue that we do have a perception of self which is an unchanging core or essence, but we shall not discover whether or not such consciousness is immortal until our physical body dies. This sense of self has no identity in terms of personality, is not perceived through thought and is the conscious awareness of our "being" (soul awareness).

Somehow, our brain seems to combine these two diverse forms of experience, to conclude that our self has a central core with a solid, self-image or personality. We combine the timeless, selfless reality of our essence as "being" with the psychophysical experience arising through the activity of our human organism within the context of space and time. The outcome is that the brain conceives that we are an animal with a personal nature in the form of an internal subject, directing our life and making our decisions.

If this is the case, how are we to make sense of our existence? We live our lives within the context of time and space, through the medium of a personality subject to the influence of what we have called "non-being". This disrupts the order of the brain and affects its ability to think rationally, leading to the illusory perception of an internal subject directing our lives. Man's essence as "being" has no identity in terms of personality and is a selfless, universal phenomenon. It would appear that if man is to live authentically, he needs to develop a personality which reflects his true spiritual nature and deals with 'self-experience' in a selfless way. If this is the case, what does it mean to be oneself? Is the question paradoxical?

What it means to be Oneself

If the "Ground of Being" is the source of my life force within the universal flux, then it is rational to assume a relationship between this reality and the genetic make-up of my body. If this is the origin of the soul, or spirit, and is the energy which gives life and form to the body, it must influence all the cells that constitute that body and which are, in themselves, packets of energy. It is impossible to conceive how these energy systems interact to create living matter and consciousness, but not too far-fetched to suggest that the "Ground of Being" and the soul or spirit are connected and can interact to exert an influence over the workings of the different organs of the body, including the brain.

Whilst I do not visualise the soul as an inner subject, controlling the operations of the brain and mind, I do conceive of the possibility of the soul as a facilitator, interacting with the ground of its origin to influence and regulate other energy systems within the body. Soul awareness could lead to synchronicity between the "Ground of Being" and the body that manifests itself as heart-felt feelings and intuitive thought.

We have suggested that the "Ground of Being" embraces a form of creative intelligence and energy that far exceeds human understanding. It would seem reasonable to suggest that the creative energy which has given life to form is not without purpose and that life itself is not meaningless. It is up to each of us to discover a personal vision which gives a sense of purpose and meaning to our own life.

Could it be that our purpose in life is to develop and use the gifts or talents which are encoded within our unique genetic blueprint, in order to serve our fellow man in a spirit of unconditional love? Is it the quest of each individual, through a process of synchronicity with the universal flux, to discover the role to which they are best suited, and to discover the person that they have the potential to be, within space and time? Is this not tantamount to suggesting that the purpose of life is to be oneself? If there is a purpose to my existence, it must be integrally linked to the interaction between the "Ground of Being", my personal sense of "being" in terms of body, mind and spirit, and the "being" of my fellow human beings and other creatures.

In Chapter 3 we concluded that rational behaviour recognised the irrational nature of psychological time that focused on an illusory self-image. We represented this diagrammatically as follows Figure 5.1:

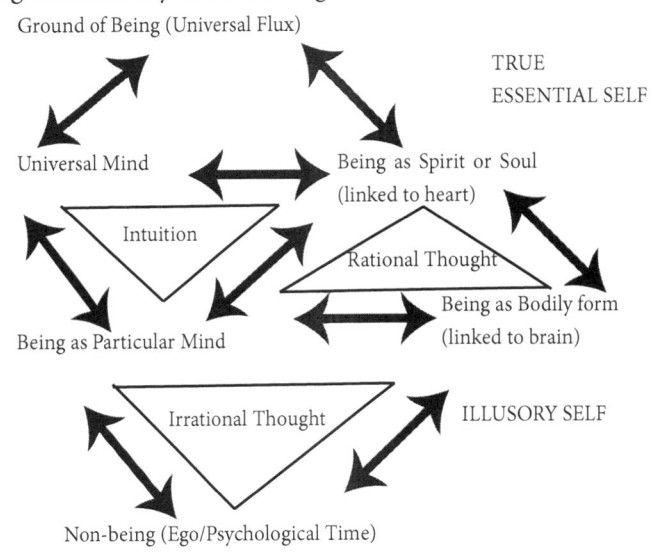

Ground of Being (Universal Flux)

TRUE ESSENTIAL SELF

Universal Mind ⟷ Being as Spirit or Soul (linked to heart)

Intuition

Rational Thought

Being as Bodily form (linked to brain)

Being as Particular Mind

Irrational Thought

ILLUSORY SELF

Non-being (Ego/Psychological Time)

We suggested that, when man is free of psychological time, there is a synchronicity between the energy fields which give form to the individual and the "Ground of Being" with a related exchange of energy and information. When our consciousness is tuned to the present moment, our particular mind field is able to interact with a source of intelligence which is beyond our understanding. This intelligence interacts with our organism in some way which by-passes conscious thought to create a phenomenon we call intuition, a form of energy exchange manifested as thought and feelings. When the individual experiences this state of existence, a state of soul awareness, could this be what it means to "experience oneself"? Is this an experience of one's true, essential self in contrast to the illusory self-image, the product of psychological time?

When we consider the whole concept of what it means to be oneself, what implications does this have for the concept of free will? If we make a decision unconsciously it will not be free because it will be a conditioned response related to 'the range of units' that contribute toward our sense of 'I' at that moment, in relation to the factors which are perceived to be significant in a given situation. If we make decisions from a perspective of love or intuition, however, are these free, or are they prompted by a universal order, or creative intelligence, that inspires a spontaneous response which over-rides reasoned choice? When we act out of love we intuitively know what we must do, the need for conscious thought is unnecessary and so the concept of free will would appear to be irrelevant.

Our decisions appear to be conditioned by constraints that are a function of many variables exerting influences in a particular situation. Our response is a function of the dynamic situation existing between "being" and "non-being" at that one moment and could well differ for the same individual at different moments in time, depending on their state of awareness. If you stop to consider the whole concept of the individual and free will, one has to ask if the question is even relevant because it implies the existence of a separate self, an entity that is capable of making decisions, when we have already suggested that our real essence is process. It would appear that to truly experience oneself we need to flow spontaneously and intuitively with the process of "being" in the "now" moment. Conscious decision-making is a brain-dominated activity which takes place within time and space and is susceptible to psychological time.

We, as human beings, should live in a way that promotes the common good of the whole of humanity and does not focus solely on our perceived personal needs. This is analogous to the role of cells contributing to the life and health of a living body. Each cell has a specific purpose, needed if the organism is to be healthy, and when cells do not function according to their purpose the organism becomes diseased. When you look at humanity today you cannot help but feel its state of health is not very good. One of the main afflictions affecting its health is anxiety.

Anxiety

It is conceivable that fear and anxiety are phenomena, or states, which are perceived when the particular mind is operating under the influence of the ego, in preference to the soul. When the mind is still, or involved in productive activity related to the 'being-mode' of existence, there is no trace of psychological time and we experience our essential self. This results in a peaceful state which is free of fear and anxiety.

However, it is difficult to live in a permanent state free from psychological time, and when we slip back into this mode of living we lose awareness of our essential self and come under the influence of the ego. The ego and essential self are diametrically opposed, the former being a divisive, illusory creation of the mind and the latter a function of our "being" which seeks fulfilment through a unified relationship with other living creatures and with the ground of its origin. During psychological time the particular mind loses awareness of its sense of spiritual "being", its link with universal mind and intuitive insight, and its sense of connection with the "Ground of Being". Could it be that it is this loss of soul awareness that manifests itself as anxiety and fear?

If we return to our analogy with the electric circuit we can view the situation as follows:

Power source (Being-itself)

Switch (Life connection)

Variable Resistor

(Pyschological time)

Light bulb
(Spiritual centre/state of mind)

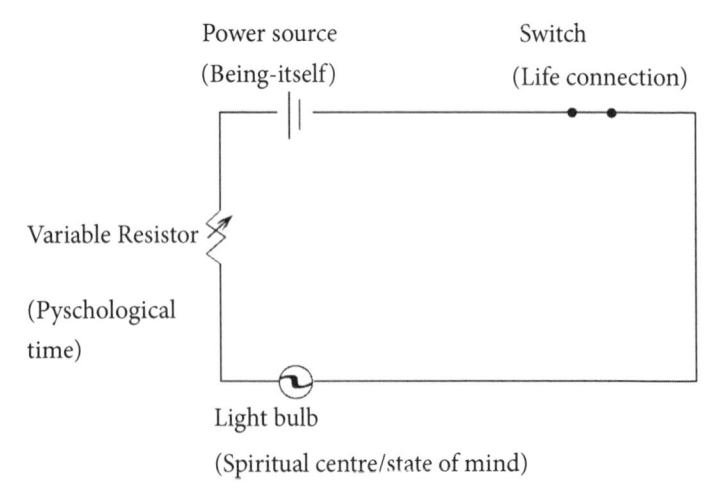

Figure 5.2

Outside psychological time, life is experienced in the 'being mode' and the resistance of the ego is negligible. The current of spiritual "being" is strong and the light shines brightly radiating joy, peace of mind and serenity. The situation within the context of psychological time creates a high internal resistance to the flow of spiritual energy. This results in the creation of a foreboding sense of inner darkness, an absence of peace of mind and the presence of anxiety or fear.

The ego is our sense of psychophysical attachment to those things that are a part of our environment: our body, memories, ideas, opinions, property, reputation, status, other people etc. An attachment to these gives each of us a form of identity, an illusory impression of who we are. Most people believe that it is a stable, authentic conception commensurate with reality and they do not realise that it is an illusory creation of the brain, a mask that they wear. Indeed, "mask" implies that they only have one persona when, in reality, we are all inclined to wear different masks at different times, depending on circumstances and the role we are playing (e.g. parent, teacher, policeman, bank manager etc.). If, as we go about our daily lives, our 'role-play' lacks conscious awareness of spiritual "being" our behaviour may not encourage a bond of unity with others and may cause division.

The problem is that if we live unconsciously, we spend much of our life within the realm of psychological time and become preoccupied with the ego. The ego is obsessed with the multitude of attachments which give it a sense of identity and accepts the loss of any of these will diminish its value or worth. It is keen to hold on to, and make secure, all that gives substance to its illusory self and when the individual lives from this perspective connection is lost with the essential self. This results in a loss of awareness of spiritual "being" that manifests itself as anxiety and fear. Indeed, the unfettered ego can never gain enough security and strives to gain more and more money, success, adulation, or whatever it perceives will enhance its sense of self-worth and make it more secure.

I believe that fear and anxiety are linked to what we see as the threat of losing the things that contribute to the sense of identity that defines the illusory self, the 'I'. It is obsessive concern with ego preservation that leads to the loss of spiritual connection, or energy, with the manifestation of anxiety or fear. If the threat is explicit, this manifests itself as fear and we can take action to try and deal with the fear. If, for example, we suspect that we are being burgled, that a robber is in our house, an initial feeling of anxiety, caused by the perception of a noise downstairs, is translated into fear as we recognise the object of our anxiety. We can then decide what sort of action to take, whether to phone the police, confront the burglar or maybe even hide from him. It would appear that fear has a definite cognitive focus, something that can be expressed in terms of thought and responded to, whereas anxiety has no recognisable object and is more nebulous.

Anxiety then, is an existential condition which is brought about by the ego's continual search for security. It is the outcome of brain-induced activity which creates an illusory entity (within psychological time) which is seeking the pursuit of a state (security) which does not exist in reality. It is a condition in which the individual is unconscious of their true sense of "being" which results in a depletion of spiritual energy.

Tillich[3] says that, while fear leads to measures that can deal with the object of fear, anxiety cannot do so because it has no object. He says that it is biologically useless and produces self-defying behaviour. This is true because it has its origin in the ego, an illusory self-concept which gives the individual a false sense of who they are (i.e. self-defying with respect to the essential self). The presence of "nonbeing" within the ego is perceived at soul level, and the resultant interaction of the different forms of energy manifests itself in the form of anxiety. This is related to the insecurity of the illusory self as it struggles for survival at the expense of the essential self.

If the different personae we adopt in life are strongly influenced by the constraints of psychological time our behaviour will be egocentric and potentially divisive. Our relationships with other people will be shallow and lack the cohesive quality and depth of those which are based on love. The outcome will be a lack of trust and empathy, with its related insecurity, leading to a feeling of dissonance both within the individual and between the individual and other people. This may be experienced as an insidious angst or uneasiness that remains hidden unless it can be given conceptual expression in terms of fear, or in terms of the recognition of dysfunctional behaviour that is inconsistent with the 'being-mode' of existence. If the individual gains some insight into the root cause, and is able to translate it into thought, it is possible to restore the dynamic balance toward "being" by a change in behaviour, but while it remains hidden, the anxiety persists.

We have already considered that "being" has biological, cognitive and spiritual dimensions and Tillich suggests that these are related to different forms of anxiety.

The Anxiety of Fate and Death

Before we discuss the anxiety of fate and death it may be interesting to speculate about what might happen when we die. In his book, 'The Visionary Human', Drury believes that, without incorporating mystical and paranormal data into our paradigm of reality, our attempts at an integrated world-view will be shallow and incomplete. He discusses examples where subjects of near death experiences (NDEs) report a state of consciousness that seems to be the source of their real identity, but which is far less restricted than what they experience in their normal physical state. This would be consistent with what we have said about the limitations imposed by physical existence, whereby the brain filters information passing through our normal, restricted sensory channels.

If NDEs are genuine experiences of reality this might suggest that some form of existence may be possible beyond the limits of our physical mortality. We have suggested that our essential self is a function of spiritual "being" which has its origin in the "Ground of Being" and experiences a synchronous relationship with particular mind and universal mind. When we die physically we know that our body undergoes a process of decay, but is it possible for the energy fields which gave rise to spirit and particular mind to co-exist in another dimension and experience a synchronous relationship with universal mind? This would lead to a form of existence that was rational (free from ego because the brain no longer exists), all-knowing and embraced an enhanced perception of unity with the "Ground of Being".

Survivors of NDEs attempt to describe an experience which appears to contain these elements but, because the experience is ineffable, they struggle to find suitable language to express or define it. Could it be that NDEs point to the fact that physical death may not be the end and that other aspects of our "being" continue to exist within another dimension? What I consider to be significant is that, when subjects of NDEs return to their physical existence, they have an unshakeable conviction of the central nature and importance of love and a loss of the fear of death.

So what is the fear of death? Tillich[4] has suggested that it determines the element of anxiety in every fear, that it is the threat of "non-being", but what does this mean in concrete terms? I believe that the fear of death is related to the perceived loss of the separate 'I'. The irrational mind, under the influence of the ego, identifies itself with the physical body, its perceived personal characteristics and its possessions. These give it a focus for its sense of identity. When the particular mind is given this irrational focus it loses cognizance of a rational awareness of its true nature as a function of spirit. This cuts it off from the influence of spiritual "being" and universal mind, with the manifestation of anxiety and fear. It would appear that the anxiety of fate and death is related to the anticipated death of the ego which is inevitable with physical death.

Paradoxically, the death of the ego is what leads to a sense of peace and the loss of anxiety and fear. For example, when the ego of an individual perceives a threat, it automatically retreats into psychological time to defend the perception of 'me', and as we discussed previously, this reduces soul awareness. If the ego anticipates the immanent exposure of its inauthentic behaviour, the brain works furiously within the context of psychological time to protect this illusory phantom, and in the process, generates negative energy (non-being), the intensity of which cuts it off even more from the power of spiritual "being". This results in a feeling of intense anxiety which grips the individual and can lead to an impairment of cognitive function.

However, if its inauthentic behaviour is exposed, the ego can vanish (or die) temporarily and the relationship between brain, soul, particular mind and universal mind can become synchronous as the individual re-establishes contact with his essential self. This is why we hear of situations where an individual has experienced a sense of relief and peace of mind (a loss of anxiety) when his wrongdoing has been brought to light and acknowledged. However, the apparent death of the ego is only temporary as it can soon resurrect itself within the process of psychological time.

Fear and anxiety arise when the separate 'I' perceives that it may not be able to deal with certain situations, especially those which involve suffering or pain. We do not know what fate has in store for us and the question arises as to how we should approach the possibility of any unpleasant experience.

Alan Watts[5] points out that there are two ways of understanding experience: to compare it with the memories of other experiences and so try to name or define it (the process of ego or psychological time); or to be aware of it as it is (the process of the essential self, operating in the "now" moment). The ego is attached to pleasure, of which it seeks more and is averse to pain from which it tries to escape. The essential self is aware of whatever is the present experience. If this is pleasurable, or joyful, it seeks to enjoy the moment but, when the moment passes, it does not seek to hold on to it through the process of memory and lets it go. If the process is painful it experiences the pain and tries to absorb it. When pain is inescapable any attempt by the mind to resist or escape only makes it worse.

Watts[6] suggests that when you live fully in the present moment you bring into play new powers of adaptation to life which literally absorb pain and insecurity. The mind discovers that resistance and escape, the "I" process, is a false move because pain is inescapable and resistance, as a defence, only makes it worse. All the mind can do is remain stable and absorb the pain in the same complete, unselfconscious way it experiences joy. When we do not try to separate ourselves from the experience, we operate in the 'being mode' and experience life in the "now" moment, from the perspective of our essential self.

What are we saying? We appear to be saying that fear of suffering is related to the process of psychological time where the separate "I" is anticipating pain and trying to escape from it. You may argue, quite legitimately, that physical pain and suffering are not illusory conditions of human existence, that they are very real and are not born of an imagination which wants to live in the past or future. Physical pain is a part of reality which is very unpleasant and nobody, unless they are a masochist (in which case they experience pain as pleasure), wants to experience it if it can possibly be avoided.

However, fear is still a function of the separate 'I' that

sees itself to have an individual body sensitive to pain. It is true that the body is sensitive and the separate 'I' strives, if possible, to remove itself from a situation which is a potential source of physical or emotional pain. Extreme fear and intense anxiety are very uncomfortable feelings and it is sensible to try if possible to escape from their hold over us. It is natural, sensible and a function of our survival instinct to try and remove or free ourselves from situations which are unpleasant and life-threatening, if at all possible. This becomes a difficult issue when the release of anxiety and fear has repercussions for the safety and well-being of others.

During the last war many people were subjected to torture as a means of extracting information. We cannot begin to imagine the extreme levels of anxiety and fear experienced as each separate 'I' sought to extricate itself from what was an impossible situation. Many succumbed quickly to their fears and anxieties, providing information which led to the suffering and demise of others but spared them the agony of physical pain. A number of brave people sacrificed their own life rather than jeopardise the lives of others, as they discovered a level of courage which enabled them to face and overcome their anxiety and fear.

Somehow, they were able to ignore the demands of the separate 'I' and to demonstrate love in the truest sense by recognising their shared "being" with others. This was a commitment to love as an ultimate concern, a manifestation of true faith which inspired true courage. This was a response of the essential self that was able to overcome the negativity of the "non-being" of its own ego and that of the collective ego of those who perpetrated evil. Could it be that when our commitment to love is so strong, we are able to access the 'courage to be' that enables us to remain stable, absorb pain and adapt to any situation, even unto death?

The Anxiety of Emptiness and Meaninglessness

Tillich[7] says that spiritual self-affirmation occurs during every moment where man lives creatively in the various spheres of meaning. He affirms himself as receiving and transforming reality creatively. This is consistent with Tillich's view that "Being-itself", the "Ground of Being", is itself living creativity.

It would therefore appear that man must seek to live his life creatively in accordance with his perceptions of reality, bearing in mind that these may change with time because reality is not static but in the process of evolution. Logically he must create a framework of values which expresses what is of ultimate concern to him, guides his behaviour and gives meaning to his life. This is the definition of faith as propounded by Tillich and discussed in a previous chapter where I suggested that the only viable ultimate concern was that of love as a commitment to shared "being".

Man must try to live his life according to values which promote the cause of love, but he will not always be successful because reality is such that his "being" is always in a dynamic relationship with "nonbeing" (ego). He should aim to stay mindful of those values which give concrete expression to his ultimate concern and use them to give his life a sense of direction. Without this, there is a danger that his thoughts will be dominated by the concerns of the ego, which are far from ultimate, and his life will be subjected to forms of emptiness and meaninglessness.

Tillich[8] defines the term meaninglessness as the absolute threat of "non-being" to spiritual self-affirmation and the term emptiness as the relative threat to it. Meaninglessness is anxiety about the loss of an ultimate concern, of a meaning which gives overall meaning. As we discussed earlier, many people have an unconditional concern (e.g. money, fame) which they perceive to be ultimate and they create a framework of values in relation to that concern. When this 'faith' is revealed to them as idolatrous, the perceived meaning they attached to it disappears leaving a feeling of emptiness which they try to fill with a new 'ultimate' concern. When they discover that this, too, is less than ultimate, they are driven from one form of activity to another because the perceived meaning in each disappears. They try everything but nothing leads to fulfilment and the emptiness experienced, in flitting from one activity to another, leads to meaninglessness.

It should be apparent to the reader, by now, that the root cause of idolatrous faith and meaninglessness is pre-occupation with the ego and its concern with the illusory 'I'. Any concern which traps the individual in psychological time leads to a lack of awareness of spiritual "being" or a perception of anxiety, in this case, the anxiety of meaninglessness.

Absolute faith is about the ultimate concern of living a life which accords with the process of shared "being" or love. Man aspires to this ideal but his faith is not absolute because he is susceptible to the influence of "non-being" in the form of psychological time. Consequently, there will always be an element of doubt, an aspect of "non-being", and this is something with which he has to learn to live and is part of the spiritual journey. As mentioned earlier, one of the problems with faith is translating the spiritual ideal of love into appropriate forms of behaviour within the context of space and time. We have established that our perception of reality is wrapped up in a process of change with consequent evolutionary change to our thoughts and concepts. We have acknowledged the surreptitious influence of psychological time on our ability to think in a rational way and suggested that there is a need to respond intuitively to situations which allow heart and mind to correspond synchronously.

What of the man who is unable or unwilling to think for himself, who feels insecure when given the freedom to shape his own destiny and define his own values? He may rely on the teachings and influence of others to determine his values and behaviour, and may feel secure within a large group of people who share the same beliefs. This community, whether it is a religious or political organisation, or local gang, will give him a sense of identity and his loyalty and commitment to the particular organisation will appear sacred. It will provide a framework for his existence and, although there may be elements or aspects of the organisation or its constitution which may not resonate authentically with the individual, these will be suppressed or overlooked because the uncertainty caused by reflection on these elements would undermine his sense of self integration.

The individual assumes an identity related to the collective ego of the particular organisation and when its values or constitution are called into question, elements of "non-being" (ego reaction) arise in the individual. Where issues are raised which question beliefs held by the group that do not resonate authentically with the individual, and have consequently been repressed, these will lead to great anxiety because they threaten self-integration (they create the negative energy of "non-being" which repels spiritual "being" and separates the individual from the perception of the essential self). These issues will meet with fanatical opposition because the alternative leads to a collapse of the foundation of the belief system. His fixed views would be exposed to doubt and their denial would lead to a breakdown of that which provides him with a false sense of security, leading to despair.

People who are religious fundamentalists defend their extreme viewpoints with certitude. They are intolerant of queries or points raised by "outsiders" that question the validity of their claims, which they defend by reference to a higher authority (e.g. Church, Bible, Koran). They are unable to have a full encounter with reality and indulge in extreme forms of behaviour such as the 'Spanish Inquisition' or, in most recent times, suicide bombing.

The Anxiety of Guilt and Condemnation

"Nonbeing" also threatens man's moral self-affirmation which requires him to account for his actions and produces anxiety which, in relative terms, is the anxiety of guilt; or in absolute terms, the anxiety of self-rejection or self-condemnation.

Man has the freedom to make of himself what he will and, if he tries to be true to his essential self, he will avoid emptiness and meaninglessness in their extreme forms. However, man will not be able to escape totally the effects of "non-being" which is personalised in the ego and it is easy to see how a conflict of interests between the ego and the wider good can lead to guilt and anxiety. Also, existential doubt can cloud moral issues and create 'grey areas' which can undermine moral self-affirmation. In such cases, the individual can feel guilty about his doubt whilst, at the same time, his guilt is undermined by doubt.

Guilt is normally associated with what we call conscience, but what is the nature of this phenomenon which is frequently ridiculed by those who are dismissive of the spiritual dimension?

The Nature of Conscience

Man's "being" gives rise to an intuitive understanding that love is the fundamental value of life. This may be considered as *a priori*, something he perceives ontologically, a pre-logical, pre-moral understanding which exists beyond thought and is part of the natural order of the universe. If this is true then man gives meaning to life when he seeks to align the psychophysical activity of his existence in time and space with this spiritual imperative.

The individual who has developed a sensitive awareness of the spiritual dimension can sense intuitively how he should respond to a given situation, but what inspires this intuitive imperative? Theism would consider this to be brought about through the agency of a separate being (i.e. a theistic God). An alternative conception may view the reality as brought about through a relationship involving energy exchange at an unconscious spiritual level, between the individual and the "Ground of Being".

Could it be that conscience reveals itself through a

process which involves the interaction between unconscious spiritual energy and the energy fields related to the heart and mind? Is it the case that dissonance between these forms of energy initially manifests itself as a form of anxiety that finds expression intuitively in the experience of guilt? Furthermore, is it possible for the individual to experience different forms of guilt, which arise from different sources, and could be considered to be either authentic or inauthentic?

Maybe it is possible to experience different forms of guilt that arise from two unconscious sources alluded to by Frankl: unconscious spirituality; or unconscious instinctuality, which is a function of psychophysical factors. Conscience could be considered to function authentically when it is related to unconscious spirituality but lack authenticity when its origin is unconscious instinctuality.

What does this mean? Where psychophysical activity is incongruous with love, this may cause dissonance within a relationship leading to estrangement. Conscience, as a response of unconscious spirituality, perceives a change in the dynamics of related energy fields and responds intuitively, through authentic guilt, to make the individual aware that his behaviour is inappropriate. This leads to a process of soul-searching, whereby synchronicity between the particular mind of the individual and universal mind reveals an intuitive awareness of action which needs to be taken in a given situation. When this is perceived and responded to intelligently, it leads to a restoration of inner peace and harmony and a healing of relationships.

However, unconscious instinctuality is linked to the psychological and physiological factors that relate to psychological time (the 'id' that drives the ego). Where an individual ego is subject to the influence of another ego, or egos, attachments are formed which can exert a strong hold that binds or imprisons the individual within collective ego boundaries. This form of relationship is not based on love and is influenced by the relative strength of individual egos, or by the collective ego within a group or organisation, that seeks to control or possess (e.g. certain extreme religious groups). The outcome is that the individual wishes to please the controlling ego(s) and feels subject to what is, in effect, emotional blackmail. It becomes easy for the individual to feel a sense of angst when the controlling ego(s) expresses dissatisfaction with the way he behaves and this leads to the manifestation of inauthentic guilt. This is the product of a pseudo-conscience which has its origin in unconscious instinctuality and is not an authentic response to the spiritual imperative of love.

Some people may argue that both a conscience and a pseudo-conscience are irrational responses to experience. It may be true of the latter but perhaps an authentic conscience is a rational (or pre-logical) process, in spite of the fact that it is not the outcome of conscious reason or thought. For this to be true, it would be necessary to show that conscience inspires action which is consistent with reason. Where conscience throws light on estrangement and inspires a response of love in action, then I would contend that this is consistent with the voice of reason and therefore rational. In contrast, it is action taken as an outcome of pseudo-conscience, from the perspective of the illusory ego that is irrational.

How does man respond to his conscience? It will depend on what he considers to be of ultimate concern to him, or what we have defined as his faith. If his faith is idolatrous, his response to conscience will not be authentic and he may not even recognise it to be the call of the transcendent. He may choose to suppress its influence and shut it out altogether. If man recognises love as an ultimate concern and has conditioned himself to be aware of the spiritual dimension, he is able to develop a relationship with the unconscious that stirs him to respond to situations through intuitive action which is consistent with love. When man has failed to develop this relationship, his sensitivity to the unconscious stirring of his spiritual nature is underdeveloped and is easily overwhelmed by the demands of the conscious mind. He may be aware of a distant murmur, in the recesses of his unconscious mind, but is conditioned to respond to the more immediate call of his ego.

In the case of pseudo-conscience, man is trapped in a collective ego boundary where he becomes subjected to the control of the dominant factor, whether this is in the form of an individual ego or a collective ego that gives expression to some dogmatic directive. He is cut off from soul awareness, experiences anxiety but is unable to address this authentically because his freedom to do so has been taken away and he has made himself into a prisoner. He has handed over the responsibility for the psychophysical expression of his existence to a third party. He will not experience a true sense of freedom until he is able to develop soul awareness and respond intuitively to situations. This may involve accessing the 'courage to be' in confronting the "non-being" that is present in situations where ego participation is pronounced.

Guilt and Love

Love grounds us in a relationship with "Being-itself" where we experience our essential self as part of a unified whole. The problem of existence is the loss of conscious awareness of this unity through the unconscious influence of the ego (unconscious instinctuality) which causes suffering in various forms. When we become conscious of having behaved in an unconscious way which has led to estrangement with others, we may experience the anxiety of guilt which, in extreme cases, can lead to self-condemnation. This leads to the feeling of a loss of the peaceful connection to the "Ground of Being".

However, "Being-itself" as a reality of love will always work toward drawing the individual back into its unified whole, like the shepherd who seeks to return his lost sheep to the fold. When the physical body is injured the force of nature works to heal the wounds and in the same way, "Being-itself" works to heal the wounds of separation and promote wholeness or unity.

We have established that guilt and self-condemnation arise from behaviour which causes division and separation. The individual feels separated from both "Being-itself" and the "being" of the person whom he has wronged with the subsequent manifestation of the anxiety of guilt. When this happens, the only way to resolve the problem is through the expression of contrition and the process of forgiveness.

If an individual is involved in a dispute and recognises, through the process of conscience, that he is the guilty party, the first thing he needs to do is to acknowledge his guilt and apologize. Where there is genuine regret and a desire to repair the relationship, the guilty party opens the spiritual channel which restores unity with "Being-itself". However, sometimes the injured party does not want to heal the rift because the pain and suffering is felt deeply and reconciliation is perceived to be impossible.

If this happens, the latter feels cut off from "Being-itself" by the strong, negative effect of "non-being" which suppresses the flow of spiritual energy, causing pain and a feeling of alienation. Relief from this pain and suffering will be impossible whilst the injured party remains in the grip of the ego and "non-being". Given time, they may develop a reconnection with "Being-itself" and experience a lessening of the ego's grip, leading to reconciliation at a later date. There is little the guilty party is able to achieve until such times as the injured party is able to transcend the influence of his own ego by becoming receptive to the power of "Being-itself". When this happens, the latter is able to recognise his essential self and feels able to forgive.

The question arises as to how the guilty party can cope with his guilt if the injured party will not forgive him. If he is genuinely sorry for what he has done and sincerely tries to make amends, he should feel a sense of release from his guilt and be at peace with the "Ground of Being". This implies that release from guilt and condemnation is rooted in "Being-itself", in spite of the fact that a guilty party may not be forgiven by an injured party.

What is the mechanism which leads to the release of guilt? Guilt and condemnation are responses to activity that has its roots in "non-being". Only when we encounter our real essential self in union with "Being-itself" (God), when we are free of psychological time, can we access a source of power which enables us to accept forgiveness (gain release from anxiety) and feel a sense of peace. This sense of union with the "Ground of Being" is what we have defined as love (what could be considered as 'the Love of God') and it is experienced within the "now" moment of chronological time. Guilt can only persist if we allow ourselves to remain under the influence of psychological time. If the injured party continues to live from this perspective, the guilty party cannot allow this cloud to cast a shadow over his own existence.

Man's Quest for Meaning and an Ultimate Concern

Frankl[9] believes that man is characterised by his "search for meaning," and that where he fails to find meaning and purpose he exists in an "existential vacuum", because *"he knows neither what he must do nor what he should do, or for that matter, what he wishes to do."* Being human means responding to life situations, and the questions they ask, in a way that fulfils meaning.

Frankl[10] suggests that it is by virtue of, what he calls, the *pre-reflective ontological self-understanding*, or what is called "the wisdom of the heart," that man knows that being human means being responsible for fulfilling the meaning potential inherent in a given life situation. He says[11] that pre-reflective ontological self-understanding really consists of two aspects: a "pre-logical understanding of being" and a "pre-moral understanding of meaning." What could he mean?

In Chapter 3 we asked the question whether, or not, spiritual intuition is rational, or whether the terms "pre-logical" or "pre-rational" were more appropriate. Authentic intuition is not based on conscious reason but can be shown, retrospectively, to be consistent with reason. It is a process that operates prior to logic or reason and therefore is pre-logical or pre-rational. What inspires this unconscious form of communication?

It appears to me that man is unconsciously aware of an energy link that connects him to the "being" of others and the "Ground of Being". Could this be what Frankl means by a "pre-logical understanding of being"? Could it also be the case that, at an unconscious spiritual level, man senses that this connection has a significant role to play in his quest for meaning which could be described as a "pre-moral understanding of meaning"? A blending of these phenomena leads to pre-reflective ontological self-understanding which manifests itself as intuition. This represents a state whereby man's "being" experiences a connection with the "Ground of Being" and Universal Mind.

Each life situation confronting us places a demand on us, asks a question of us which requires a response. This presents us with different possibilities in terms of how we respond to a given situation. Our psychophysical response will be influenced by our degree of awareness of the spiritual dimension, our openness to heart-felt intuition and the conceptual structures and paradigms that are at our disposal. It will be a function of the values which give meaning to our life. As we have already discussed, if our values are the creation of an idolatrous faith they will lack spiritual meaning and may lead to a feeling of emptiness or an existential vacuum.

Frankl[12] suggests that there is ultimate meaning in the universe, that one's life has meaning but that ultimate meaning is beyond comprehension. What does this mean? He seems to be saying that the universe has ultimate meaning which we call love, a phenomenon related to our essence as "being" and its relationship to "Being-itself". This is a spiritual phenomenon that cannot be expressed in words and is incomprehensible in terms of thought. It is impossible to define spiritual meaning in terms of thought and express this in terms of some unchanging universal law.

Life can be seen as a journey, the meaning of which is to live in a way which attempts to actualise spiritual reality. Meaning is not conveyed in words but through heart-felt action which connects at the level of our "being". Meaning can only be expressed through action which is a live response to what is felt, by the heart, to be necessary in the moment. Action in the service of love is the ultimate meaning of life and of the universe. Words can only point toward a reality which is active and requires an active response to provide authentic meaning.

What man needs to ask himself is whether his answers to life's questions arise from an ontological, spiritual source, or whether they are the outcome of psychophysical activity operating in isolation. If the influence is not of a spiritual nature, if it does not arise from a spiritual perspective of love, then the meaning it expresses may lack authenticity.

Overcoming Despair

Tillich says that the different forms of anxiety are existential and contribute to the situation of despair which means to be without hope. Frankl[13] refers to the feeling of meaninglessness in terms of existential despair or spiritual distress, which arises in an existential vacuum where there is a lack of meaning.

When a person is in despair he is unable to affirm himself because of the power of "non-being". He has lost awareness of his soul (and the "Ground of Being") which has been diminished by the influence of psychological time, and because he is unable to recognise his true essential self, is he unable to affirm it? He realises that something is wrong but the problem is that he does not understand what, and why. He tries to confront his despair but his 'courage to be as oneself', is misdirected because he does not know who he is. He has no spiritual centre because he is driven by his own ego which is illusory, empty and without meaning.

Twenty-first century man has lost a meaningful world and a self which lives in meanings out of a spiritual centre. He has been drawn into the world of material devices, which are of his own creation, and he is bombarded by a host of distractions in terms of material goods and mass media, in a multitude of forms. It is easy for the individual to drown in a flood of distraction and it has become even more important to be able to discern what is, or is not meaningful. This becomes overwhelming for the individual who exists in an existential vacuum.

Many people today do not realise that they live their lives in the grip of "non-being". Their lack of direction and purpose causes anxiety from which they try to escape through various distractions. Modern man focuses his attention on having a good time, and making sure that he does not miss out on contemporary pleasures. He is prepared to work hard but subjects himself to the stresses and strains of the workplace with its cut-throat ethos. This takes its toll on his nervous system and leads to strained relationships which, in turn, lead to family breakdown and separation.

Much of the current gang culture reflects the need of young people for recognition and a sense of belonging unavailable within their own family. Their lack of love and attention at home has been replaced by the need for the recognition and respect of their peers, which gives them a sense of belonging and is a psychophysical form of pseudo love. Others seek to blot out the anxiety of meaninglessness by searching for thrills and excitement, through alcohol, drug abuse or joy-riding.

Tillich[14] suggests that where emptiness and meaninglessness prevail, one experiences an abyss in which the meaning of life and the truth of ultimate responsibility disappear. Those who 'peer into the abyss', have no clear view of the meaning of their life or of their responsibilities (just look at the number of dysfunctional families today). They are rudderless on the sea of life, blown this way and that by the winds of fate with no clear sense of direction. Their lives are driven under the influence of psychological time and they are at the mercy of their own ego. Where life has no meaning, values are valueless and ego strives against ego.

When an individual is really gripped by doubt and meaninglessness he is desperate to find a foundation to which he can anchor, or fix his existence. He can descend into a deep pit of despair from which he feels unable to extricate himself. Frankl makes the point that you cannot give meaning to the life of others and any attempt to impose meaning, through a set of symbols or dogma, is not the solution to the problem of radical doubt. He, who is in the grip of despair, is desperate to find what Tillich calls the "courage of despair". He is seeking a source of inner strength and guidance which will enable him to climb out of the pit. He persistently struggles to lift himself out, but his sense of security is undermined by self-doubt and a lack of direction, which continually cause him to slip and slide as he cannot find a firm foothold.

If he refuses to give in to the sense of despair (or embraces "the courage of despair", which is the acceptance of a conviction that he will somehow find the strength to overcome from within himself if he refuses to succumb to his anxiety), he comes through this dark period. His confidence grows gradually over a period of time as he discovers a form of courage which enables him to face his doubt and insecurity. The intensity of his despair begins to lessen as he gradually lifts himself out of the pit. He becomes motivated to explore the nature of a developing source of inner strength and tranquillity. He has set out on a journey in search of an ultimate concern to give meaning to his life. His spiritual quest has begun.

Once he realises that there is a source of inner strength on which he can draw, once he has come to recognise the 'power of being' that lies within him, the individual senses that there is a reality which may provide the foundation on which he can give meaning to his existence. This reality is the 'power of Being-itself', and it is this that sustains the individual and which underlies and gives strength to the courage of despair. The more he becomes aware of this reality and the more consciously he attunes to it, the more peaceful he becomes. He feels a sense of unity with something that is both within and beyond him and which calls him to seek the same relationship with his fellow man. At last he begins to recognise that a commitment to unity, or love, is what gives ultimate meaning, and he seeks to pursue a way of life which is consistent and true to this ultimate concern. He is beginning to discover the nature of faith.

Faith acknowledges that the essential self is grounded in the transcendent power of "Being-itself", it is the self-affirmation of this reality, and the 'courage to be' is an expression of this faith. It is a whole-hearted commitment to live in a way which affirms love, in spite of the threat of "non-being" in all its guises (envy, hate). This is what Tillich[15] means when he says that the 'courage to be' is an expression of faith and what "faith" means must be understood by the 'courage to be'. It is not an opinion about beliefs but a state of "being".

Both Heidegger and Sartre were of the opinion that life is a blank canvas on which man is free to paint his own portrait. However, man does not live in isolation from his fellow man and is not completely free to make decisions which may affect the happiness of others or lead to conflict. Whilst it is true that man can make of himself what he wants, he has to face the consequences of the decisions which he makes, and he needs to search the depths of his "being" to discover what gives value and meaning to his life. If he allows himself to be driven by his own ego he will not live authentically, he will not be influenced by what is of ultimate concern and his life will be spiritually empty and lack meaning. He may have a blank canvas but he must somehow keep a sense of perspective, lest he produce a portrait which is grotesque and distorted. If he wishes to avoid despair, he must be careful not to fill his existence with contents that enslave him and deprive him of the freedom that he wishes to preserve.

Love and the Participation in Divine Self-Affirmation

In Chapter 2 we discussed some of the problems we have with our perception of reality, conscious of the fact that we have a body, a physical form which is manifested by the universal flux. This is perceived by our physical senses to be an entity which is separate from the flux of life, whereas our sense of intuition suggests that there is a connection. Science is now beginning to recognise and acknowledge the fact that the essence of our body is energy, which is a part of the universal flux and linked to everything else, including other human beings. We are each a creation which appears separate but is intimately linked to everything else. Like ripples in a stream, we can be identified as separate forms but are, in reality, the patterns in the water of the stream of life.

When our mind fails to recognise the link between our form and the universal flux, it gives it a separate identity which isolates it in the form of the separate 'I'. We have to live in the real world and this involves giving ourselves an identity which recognises our different form (we are ripples which are separate from the ripples of other human beings who are, nevertheless an integral part of the flowing stream), but at the same time, we have to recognise that our essence is a shared reality which we share with mankind. We need to acknowledge the fact that we are individuals who are part of a whole, to which we are inextricably linked. If we can live from this perspective, we eliminate the ego and function as our essential self.

What does it mean to affirm oneself? We have suggested that "oneself" is not an entity but a process and so self-affirmation must be an affirmation of the process of "being". Man's self-affirmation appears to have two sides which are distinguishable but not separable.

The first side is the affirmation of the essential self that exists outside of the constraints of psychological time and must not be confused with the separate 'I'. This is what one defends against "non-being" and affirms courageously by taking "non-being" upon oneself. Paradoxically, the process of psychological time seeks to promote and confirm the reality of the illusory self but leads to the threatened loss of the essential self, and is the root cause of the different forms of anxiety and fear.

Secondly, the self is self only because it has a world, a structured universe, to which it belongs and from which it appears separated at the same time. Self and world are correlated, there is individualization and participation. Tillich[16] suggests that the identity of participation is an identity in the 'power of Being'. For the concepts of self-affirmation and courage, this means that the self-affirmation of the self as an individual self always includes the affirmation of the 'power of Being' in which the self participates. If the word "God" is used to represent the reality which gives life and form to matter, then this reality is a vital presence in all living people which transcends subjectivity and objectivity. All men and women are participants in the one reality, part of something from which they are, at the same time, separated. If I, as an individual, recognise and acknowledge this reality (God) to be my true essence then surely I cannot fail to recognise this reality in other human beings.

The main barrier to this recognition is the false sense of self we each present to the outside world. We wear a mask(s) of the ego which disguises the true face of who we really are. If everybody removed their egotistic masks then we would discover that we all have an identical face. It would be easy to love each other because it would seem as though each of us was loving himself, a further indication that this reality transcends both subjectivity and objectivity.

If, as an individual, I undertake to make communion with this reality, both in myself and others, my aim in life, is this not what Spinoza meant by participation in the divine self-affirmation? Is this not an affirmation of Being-itself? Is this not truly an ultimate concern and the authentic foundation of faith?

We live in a troubled world and there is only one way to alleviate the suffering and sense of alienation which is the reality for so many people. We have to look beyond the masks that people wear and recognise the divine reality which lies hidden beneath. By developing a conscious awareness of our own behaviour and attempting to live under the influence of the divine reality, we shall begin to create a self which is motivated by love to break down the barriers of division and separation, and create a more unified world. This will not be an easy task and will require vitality and courage.

Vitality and Courage

Courage is the readiness to face up to fear and anxiety in their different forms. I think that it is the function of a vitality that arises as a consequence of a commitment to values which define what is perceived to be of ultimate concern to the individual.

The more vital strength a being has the more it is able to affirm itself in spite of the dangers announced by fear and anxiety. True self-affirmation is not a thing of the ego, it is affirmation of "Being-itself". To my mind, a person's spiritual vitality is a function of the level of commitment he makes to the acknowledgement of the common spiritual source from which we all derive. Therefore, love and compassion will feature strongly in the behaviour of somebody who has genuine self-affirmation. They are therefore likely to possess more vital strength than somebody who does not possess these qualities and be unconcerned with the drives of the ego (e.g. enlightened individuals like Jesus or the Buddha).

We discussed earlier the courage shown by individuals under torture, how they were able to suppress the demands of the separate 'I' and behave in a way which acknowledged their shared "being" with others whom they refused to betray. Authentic courage would appear to be an expression of what is truly ultimate, coming from deep within the individual as a response to what gives ultimate spiritual meaning. Tillich would say that it comes from the spiritual soul in which vitality and intentionality (the relation to meanings) are united.

Tillich[17] contrasts this type of courage with the vitality shown in Nazi Germany, directed into a political system that attacked most of the values of the western world. He suggests that the spirit was replaced by intellect and thus the spiritual soul in which vitality and intentionality are united was missing. One cannot deny the courage of the German soldiers who fought bravely and tenaciously for, what was for them, a cause of ultimate concern. Their faith, their ultimate concern was a commitment to the Fatherland and nothing else mattered.

They fought for a cause based on a jingoistic ideology which was of the brain and intellect and, consequently was a function of the collective ego of a nation. Tillich suggests that this was a barbarian courage with its roots in the mind, was divisive and had no spiritual core, which was probably one of the reasons why it failed. Could it not be the case that the perceived ultimate concern of patriotism was indeed an idolatrous faith?

What are we to make of the courage of the modern day suicide bomber who kills both himself and other innocent victims in the name of Allah, Mohammed and Islam? One could argue that his actions are a response to his faith, an ultimate concern which gives meaning to his life. He looks at the way the Western world behaves, its materialistic values, its hypocrisy and he sees that there is corruption in high places. He feels that fellow Muslims in the world are exploited and do not generally share the material benefits enjoyed by Western countries that appear to have few spiritual values.

Whilst it is easy to relate to his sense of injustice and his desire to change the status quo, and create a world that is more God-centred, it is difficult to understand the manifestation of an ultimate concern which utilises terror tactics and seeks to cause suffering. Is this behaviour likely to lead to the development of a world that reflects the realisation of what is truly ultimate? It seems to me that this form of faith is also idolatrous, a product of 'psychological time' rather than of the soul.

Who or what is the god that is inspiring and motivating

the courage of the suicide bomber? What is the ultimate concern which seeks to cause suffering and separation? Is it a truly spiritual reality, rooted within the soul of the individual? Does it lead to peace and joy? It appears to me that it is a response of the ego, an illusory self that is deluded into thinking that such behaviour will lead to martyrdom, that the individual will be transported straight to paradise where he or she will be treated like a celebrity and bestowed with all manner of gifts and honours.

Courage as a Commitment to Love

If courage is the self-affirmation of "being" in spite of "non-being" what does this mean in practical terms? We discussed earlier the courage of the prisoner who, when subjected to torture, is prepared to suffer rather than betray a fellow human being. Surely the 'courage to be' is an unequivocal commitment to "being" and its manifestation in others, a commitment to love, a spiritual imperative that one might define as 'The Will to Be'. There is a need for mankind to be united by a common will to a common meaning which I would call "The will to Love". This is the power of "Being-itself", operating within the individual to confront the "non-being" which is present within his own ego and that of others around him.

The problem we face in life is that we lose the conscious awareness of our commitment to "being", and when this happens we are susceptible to our own egocentricity and the influence of "non-being". This undermines our spiritual centre and can lead to the development of negative emotions such as anger or greed. Our sense of separation from others, or estrangement, is an indication that love is absent and this can lead to a lack of conviction in our 'courage to be'. When we recognise the signs we need to return to a conscious awareness of the "Ground of Being" and re-establish a connection with our true self. "Non-being" recedes and a sense of peace returns as we regain contact with our spiritual centre.

Anxiety, whether it be related to fate, death, emptiness and meaninglessness, or guilt and self-condemnation is a function of psychological time (non-being). Self-affirmation recognises this fact and strives to be mindful of a state of soul awareness which is cognizant of our true nature as "being", a commitment to which requires that an individual love his neighbour as himself. The more a person aspires to this ideal, the greater is his 'courage to be' and the greater is his success in overcoming the anxieties and fears of life, which are ego-related.

He who makes a commitment to love his neighbour is not assured of an easy passage in life. "Non-being" manifests itself in all sorts of atrocities which are perpetrated by those who lack conscious awareness and succumb to the excesses of their wilful and vindictive egos. History bears testimony to many courageous human beings who suffered for the sake of righteousness. Commitment to" Being-itself" and love gives a sense of spiritual purpose and joy to living. Those who follow its path discover a sense of inner peace and a conviction that they will find, within themselves, the courage to face challenges with dignity. As Tillich says, courage is not without risk and the courageous individual never knows if or when he may have to pay the ultimate price.

When we talk about Providence we are not talking about

a Being who intervenes to remove our problems. We are talking of a reality which is the source of man's 'courage to be', in facing the trials of life.

Summary of Key Ideas

- Man's perception of his 'self' is paradoxical in so far as it can change whilst, at the same time, appear unchanging.
- The reason for this paradox can be explained by the existence of two frames of reference which are related to whether, or not, man's consciousness is trapped within psychological time.
- The changing self that we perceive is the ever-changing, physiological, mind/brain generated personality which is created within time.
- In contrast, the unchanging conception of self is felt intuitively when the mind is still. This is a perception which has no identity in terms of personality, and is essentially selfless because it is not perceived by the mind but through conscious awareness of our "being".
- Our perception of self is never constant and varies across a spectrum defined in terms of "being" and "non-being".
- We combine the timeless, selfless reality of our essence as "being" with the psychological/physiological creation of self which arises as a result of the activity of our human organism within the context of space and time.
- To truly experience oneself one needs to flow

spontaneously and intuitively with the process of "being" in the "now" moment.
- Fear and anxiety are seen as phenomena, or states, which are perceived when the particular mind operates from the perspective of the ego, rather than of the soul.
- Anxiety is an existential condition which is brought about by the ego's continual search for security.
- The fear of death is related to the perceived loss of the separate 'I'.
- Man must seek to create a framework of values which expresses what is of ultimate concern to him and guides his behaviour, if he is to avoid a meaningless existence.
- Meaninglessness arises through preoccupation with the separate 'I' during psychological time.
- Man aspires to the ideal of absolute faith but its attainment is undermined by psychological time. Consequently the spiritual journey is characterised by a tension between faith and existential doubt.
- Religious fundamentalism is based on the premise that it is possible to describe reality in absolute terms that have been revealed to man through certain historical characters. This gives rise to the illusion that faith can be absolute and dogmatic.
- Man is in a state of despair when he is unable to recognise and affirm his true essential self. This happens when he completely loses awareness of his soul as a result of the influence of psychological time.
- We have to live in the world as we find it and give ourselves an identity but, at the same time, we have

to recognise that our essence is a reality called "being" which we share with mankind. Consequently, one's essential self is not an entity but a process and so self-affirmation must be an affirmation of the process of "being".

- Courage is the readiness to face up to fear and anxiety in their different forms. It is the function of a vitality which arises as a consequence of a commitment to values which define what is of ultimate concern to the individual.
- Authentic courage is an expression of what is truly ultimate. It comes from deep within the individual and is a response to what gives ultimate spiritual meaning.
- The 'courage to be' is the power of "Being-itself" confronting the "non-being" which is present in the ego of the individual and those of others around him. It is the 'Will to Be' or the 'Will to Love' which requires an individual to love his neighbour as himself.
- The more a person aspires to this ideal the greater is his courage to be and the greater is his success in overcoming the anxieties and fears of life which are ego-related.

CHAPTER 6.

The Nature of Genuine Religiousness and the Future of Religion

What is Religion?

Religion appears to be the attempt by man to understand and develop a relationship with reality (God) which gives meaning, security and a sense of purpose to life. However, when knowledge functions inwardly it is dangerous because thought can be trapped in the web of psychological time. When this happens a separate, illusory centre is created that seeks a relationship with something to give it substance and security. This whole process is a brain-dominated, temporal activity which involves the attempt to perceive a timeless function by an illusory entity. Because the process is temporal, and reality is momentary, it is impossible to establish a relationship between the two.

We suggested earlier that our basic essence is "being" which is related to the "Ground of Being" in a way that transcends a subject/object relationship. This is a relationship that we share with all mankind such that, in reality, each individual is a selfless self. However, this is not what is perceived through our sensual perceptions which the brain translates into a mental image of a separate 'I'. Our particular mind is a store of conceptual frameworks that are structured on the basis of this perception, and gives form to the identity of the individual as a primary conception of reality. It would appear that our brain is genetically programmed to operate from the perspective of the separate 'I', and it would seem that we are unconscious of this process. Our true essence is not accessible to our five senses, and consequently, our awareness of its presence is obscured by an urgent, unconditional need to satisfy the primary needs of sensual perception.

In view of what appears to be an insurmountable problem, is it possible for the human mind to establish a relationship with reality, as the "Ground of Being", that is an authentic relationship between our essence as "being" and the womb of creation which gave us life? This is not a relationship which is rooted in brain-centred activity, but comes about only when the mind is empty and the brain is not engaged in active thought. We have suggested that such a relationship is conducted through a process of intuitive insight, through an interaction of particular mind, heart and universal mind? What is insight? It must be some form of energy which inspires a certain response within the individual.

Knowledge is not what it appears to be and perceived truth is not absolute but a function of conceptual frameworks and limited sensual perceptions. Man has tried to define reality or God in terms of concepts and language. He has attempted to make explicit in knowledge a spiritual reality which he has experienced ontologically, but has failed to appreciate that reality is a flowing process that cannot be defined in finite terms. It can only be experienced in the "now" moment and cannot be described in thought. Alan

Watts likens the problem of attempting to define reality to trying to get water into neat and permanent packages.

However, man has allowed his illusory self to delude him into thinking that the truth of reality can be grasped by the mind and expressed as a body of knowledge. This has led to the development of different religions with their own brand of revealed truth and collective ego.

Religion and the Past

John Hick[1] says that before the Axial age (a period which he defines from about 800 to about 200 BCE) people did not tend to engage in critical reflection and generally accepted the conditions of their life. However, during the Axial age, individuals appeared in different parts of the world who developed insights into reality and were able to influence the societies into which they were born. They were conscious of the fact that life, as it was lived, was basically unsatisfactory and that it was necessary for individuals to change their view of reality in order to create a better society. The conception of this sense of the unsatisfactory nature of living was given the name 'sin' in the Semitic religions, and referred to as 'dukkha' by the Buddha. They refer to the same misperception of reality which is rooted in the ego and is overcome through enlightenment, which finds expression in compassion and love.

The development of the post-axial religions was directed towards enabling man to recognise this misperception and to resolve it. In western terms this meant suppressing our self-centredness and living a God-centred life, whereas from an eastern perspective, it meant recognising our true, selfless self, the atman or image of God within us, the universal Buddha nature. Living from this perspective was the source of salvation, inner peace, joy and enlightenment. It was a perspective that recognised a fifth dimension as both part of our nature and yet infinitely transcendent.

Religion and Cognitive Limitations

The fifth dimension is impossible to define in language because it is a time-less dimension (experienced in the now moment) rooted in unmanifest reality. Man has developed language as a tool to help him to interpret and understand his environment, which is part of manifest reality and has physical referents which can be observed in space and time. This fifth dimension, which has been given different names such as God, Ultimate Reality etc., is beyond human conception and can only be alluded to in a metaphorical, poetic way, much like a finger which points in a general direction but cannot specify a detailed map. Attempts to define it have led to the problem of fragmentation which divides the followers of different religions from each other. They fail to recognise that their tradition is a human response, metaphorically or poetically crafted in language that does not have a reflective correspondence with reality.

Hick[2] says,

"..there are realities external to us, but that we are never aware of them as they are in themselves, but always as they appear to us with our particular cognitive machinery and conceptual resources.."

He refers to the fourteenth century Sufi, Al-Junayd, who made the point that the colour of the water is that of its container, implying that the different traditions are the containers that give its recognizable colour, or character, to human awareness of the transcendent.

Mystics from all traditions have experienced visions of the transcendent which have been dismissed as hallucinations, and others have experienced what is commonly referred to as cosmic consciousness. Hick asks whether these experiences are illusory, or whether they are born of moments of heightened awareness when the individual suddenly becomes receptive to dimensions that are normally inaccessible. We tend to assume that we all possess the same 'cognitive machinery', and that anything which does not resonate with our own perceptions of reality must be illusory, but is this a false assumption? Could it be that man is an evolving animal and that, at some stage in the future, he will become generally receptive to aspects of reality which, at the present time, are only experienced by a limited number of individuals?

We made the point earlier, and Hick[3] reinforces the fact, that awareness is not just a case of the environment imprinting itself upon our consciousness. The human organism is subjected to an infinite barrage of information, the majority of which is filtered by the brain, nervous system and our own conceptual frameworks. Could it be that, in altered states of consciousness, this filtering mechanism is affected in some way to allow the apprehension of information which would normally be excluded? We must not forget that man's awareness of the physical world is dependent on the physical receptors, the five senses that enable us to see, hear, feel, taste and smell, which have developed as a tool for survival. Science is aware of the electromagnetic spectrum, the way it interacts with matter and the fact that our physical receptors are able to perceive only small ranges of the spectrum. It is quite conceivable that we are unable to recognise information or signals for which we do not have the appropriate receptors. We see in nature that animals differ in their ability to respond to different stimuli, with birds of prey having enhanced visual capability, and bats able to respond to sound in a way that makes visual perception irrelevant. We must not assume that something does not exist because it is not perceived by our physical senses, or that intuition is just a product of our imagination.

Hick points out that we have more cognitive freedom with regard to the spiritual domain than with our interpretation of the physical world. The physical world forces its attention on us more directly through the five senses and we have developed comprehensive conceptual structures which enable us to survive within, and utilize the physical environment. Science has developed refined theories which offer explanations of observed physical behaviour and we tend to view these theories as absolute knowledge which expresses the truth of reality. We have already shown that this is not true, but this is not generally appreciated by the man in the street, who believes that science has all the answers and is all-knowing. Consequently we tend to believe that, in terms of the physical environment, cognitive freedom is limited and reality more clearly defined.

Hick[4] makes the valid point that what he calls the Ultimately Real can only enter our consciousness in the range of forms made possible by our own conceptual systems. I believe that because the spiritual realm is a timeless reality which can only be accessed in the "now" moment, it makes it difficult to conceptualise because this involves the activity of the brain which operates within the scale of time. There is no physical referent which can be observed directly, and the timeless nature of the phenomenon leaves it open to interpretation. This is why there is cognitive freedom in the spiritual domain and why there are so many different religions. The problem arises with the perception, within different religious traditions, that each is in sole possession of the 'truth' which has been miraculously revealed to the founder of their one true faith. In truth, different religions are different conceptions of ultimate reality which have found expression in different cultural settings.

Mysticism

Hick points out[5] that according to advaitic, vedantic Hinduism there is only one reality, the eternal changeless Brahman (could this be synonymous with what we have referred to as the universal flux or 'Ground of Being'?). Our conscious self is 'unreal' in the sense that our separate individuality (ego) arises from ignorance of our true nature (we appear to be unaware of our true nature as "being") and belongs to a stream of experience related to sense and mind (are we not referring here to psychophysical experience which gives rise to ego?) that masks the Universal Consciousness, Atman, which is our true "being" and is both individual and universal. Our conscious existence is viewed as a kind of 'dream,' (our ego is unreal and illusory) within the borders of which everything and everyone is real.

This appears to be consistent with what we have been saying about the way we misperceive reality. Our senses perceive us to be individual entities and this for us becomes a reality from which we seem unable to escape. Our mind generates concepts about the nature of reality which create an image of who we are in terms of perceived skills, talents, qualities, faults, values etc. This is a constantly changing image, played out on the screen of our mind, which seeks to provide us with a concrete, tangible conception of who we are. It is what we believe to be our conscious self, but it is unreal, illusory and fails to recognise our true nature as universal consciousness, as "being" which is both individual (our essential self) and universal. Consequently, who we perceive ourselves to be (our ego) is dream-like but, at the same time, we live this 'dream' within the context of everyday life involving real people.

Mysticism and the Issue of Sin

During the fourteenth century, when the mystic Julian of Norwich was alive, Church teaching was dominated, and still is, by its obsession with the fall and redemption of man. The Church emphasised the sinful nature of man, divine condemnation and the remission of God's anger through Christ's atoning death. This picture has dominated Christian thought ever since to the detriment of the Christian faith.

Julian clearly had a problem with this view of reality as it was inconsistent with her mystical experience. She did not experience God as a judgemental, wrathful reality but as peace and love. Her thinking was clearly at odds with that of Augustine, in so far as she did not view the fall of Adam and sin in terms of rebellious disobedience to God, but more in terms of blind unawareness.

John Shelby Spong[6] says,

"The power of Western religion has always rested on the ability of religious people to understand and to manipulate that sense of human inadequacy that expresses itself in guilt....The religious leaders of the ages learned that controlling people's behaviour rested upon exacerbating these human feelings of guilt...How could guilt be overcome?...How could human life be rescued from its fall? Those were the Questions that Christianity organised itself to answer."

He goes on to say[7],

"What is sin? It is not and never can be alienation from the perfection for which God in the act of creation had intended us, for there is no such thing as a perfect creation. Thus there was no fall into sin....A saviour who restores us to our pre-fallen status is therefore pre-Darwinian superstition and post-Darwinian nonsense. A supernatural redeemer who enters our fallen world to restore creation is a theistic myth. So we must free Jesus from the rescuer role"

Humanity is an evolving species, we are not the finished article and we shall continue to evolve along with our thought forms. Salvation is a process which comes about through the union of man's "being" with "Being-itself". It results in a state of peace and love which precludes evil and fosters our highest good. Man drifts into sin when he loses awareness of his union with" Being-itself", this is the definition of sin. It is very difficult to live within the constant awareness of "Being-itself" because our mind is distracted by the process of living in the world and all that means in terms of fulfilling all necessary tasks. If we are not careful we get drawn into the brain-dominated world of the ego and our illusory preoccupation with self-centred concerns.

One could argue that man does have a sinful nature in so far as the demands of living tend to draw his attention away from timeless reality. However, this is not a wilful disobedience which makes God angry, but a lack of awareness which is born of ignorance. I believe that the vast majority of people are conscious, within the depths of their soul, of the timeless dimension of "being" and a relationship to something which is its source. Furthermore, I believe that this source reaches out to each of us, drawing us toward it in the same way as water is drawn back toward the ocean. This search for union is what we call love and it overcomes the presence of sin by removing the sense of separation.

Myth and Metaphor

The word "myth" means different things to different people and it is generally seen as a reference to something that is not true. Myths make use of metaphorical language, they express perceived truths about reality that are difficult to express literally and therefore may appear to be semantically licentious. Problems arise when myths that express a metaphorical, poetical truth about spiritual reality are interpreted as a literal truth, causing religious disputes which lead to bloodshed. Hick[8] discusses various examples of the use and misuse of myths and how the literal interpretation of religious myths has been a cause of conflict between different religious groups. This is especially the case with regard to the ownership of religious sites whose sanctity is guaranteed by ancient myths.

The nature of religion has spawned a multitude of different myths which, no doubt, had great significance for the people who inspired them and for their contemporaries in their particular cultural setting. It could be said that some of these ancient myths still have significance today but, to my mind, this depends on the way they are interpreted. For example, early Christian writers referred to Jesus as the 'Son of God' which, according to Hick, was a familiar term throughout the ancient world. Apparently, within Judaism it was a familiar metaphor for anyone who was a special servant of God and the words 'Son of' meant 'in the spirit of'. It is not difficult to see why people viewed Jesus in this way.

They saw Jesus as a special human being whose insight into the nature of reality was so comprehensive that it made him stand out among other men. His ability to love, or relate to the "being" in others, evoked a spiritual response that came from the soul and they recognised the timeless truth in what he had to say. This man was special, he understood important truths about reality (God), God was in him, and so they referred to him as the 'Son of God'. When they put into practice the essence of his teaching on love they discovered a new dimension to life, a sense of unity and peace with each other and with reality that was the antithesis of disunity or 'sin'.

The idea was conceived that Jesus had been sent by God to free them from sin and this became linked to the Jewish preoccupation with sacrifice. Consequently, Jesus was seen as a human sacrifice to God, the Lamb of God who died for our sins. Somehow, his death was perceived to cancel out the sin of mankind and all we needed to do was accept Jesus as our Saviour. The God of Theism would then mercifully grant forgiveness. What was overlooked was the fact that when we love, we automatically break down the barrier of sin which is disunity, and restore our relationship with the "Ground of Being", which is the process of salvation.

The Christian myth begins with the Christmas Story which should in no way be interpreted literally. Writers at the time were trying to establish the birth of Jesus as a momentous occasion, the arrival of somebody with very special spiritual qualities who would provide us with insights into the nature of Reality or God. In fact, this person was so different to them, so totally at peace with Reality that they perceived a special bond which they described in terms of a Father/son relationship. This was portrayed in terms of 'the immaculate conception' in which his mother Mary, a virgin, fulfilled the human role in bringing to fruition the seed of divine intervention.

Writers at the time did not understand the biological implications of what they were writing, and this was a way of explaining the nature of his person and his qualities which were other-worldly. His humility was captured in the setting of his humble birth, and the significance of his teaching reflected in the metaphorical vision of a star that would lead all men, whether they were wise kings or humble shepherds, to find salvation in what he had to say. This Christmas story was a poetic description of the birth of a person with very special qualities who had a profound message to express about the way we should live.

Jesus was a charismatic person with an overwhelming spiritual presence. His moral teaching was profound and his message of love expressed a truth of reality which resonated in the heart and soul of his followers. Jewish religious leaders at that time were concerned that he was attracting a large following and that what he had to say conflicted with their official teaching. They saw him as a threat to their authority and sought ways to get rid of him. Jesus' appearance on the scene coincided with a volatile period in Jewish history which saw hostile revolts against Roman rule that were brutally put down. The Temple priests seized an opportunity to portray Jesus to the Roman authorities as a dangerous revolutionary and they collaborated with them in his arrest, trial and execution.

However, those people who had been close to Jesus had discovered a truly timeless, spiritual dimension to their life. They realised that the spirit which had inspired Jesus was also alive in them, it was what they shared with each other and indeed with all mankind, it was the 'power of being' (Holy Spirit?). Just as Jesus had revealed the 'courage to be', in the manner in which he lived and faced death, they too discovered that a commitment to the love of God, and their fellow man, released the power of the 'courage to be' in them. The crucifixion of their ego resulted in the resurrection of their true essential self, which they interpreted as a conviction that Jesus was alive in them, an experience of inner salvation.

The basically simple message of love, which Jesus was trying to convey to his followers, seems to have become lost in the dogmatic doctrines which started soon after his death and were perpetuated and distorted by the Church in Rome, three hundred years later. The instrument which was used to execute him as a common criminal, the cross of crucifixion, was used as a symbol to glorify his death, as the sacrifice of God's Son to God himself. The very idea that a theistic God would want to subject a son to great suffering and rejection is inconsistent with a God of love.[Personally, I find it very difficult, and always have done, to make any sense at all out of this part of the myth.]

Jesus emphasised the importance of the love of both God and one's fellow man which were central to his teaching. He was an articulate man who would have recognised the dangers to which he was subjecting himself, through the nature of his teaching. He knew that what he had to say would not be well-received by the Jewish religious leaders. He must have known that to express the truth about Reality, or God, in the terms of his perceptions and conceptions would be misunderstood within the conceptual world view of his cultural setting. He would have anticipated that his teachings would be viewed as blasphemy and that this could probably lead to his death but, in spite of this, he found inner strength, through the 'courage to be', to remain true to his essential self. He was able to take his anxieties onto himself, subjugate his ego and pursue the spiritual task which he perceived to be his destiny, no matter what the cost to his personal safety.

To say that the death and suffering of Jesus was a pre-ordained act, carried out in accordance with God's will to pay the price for man's sin is, to my mind, the product of muddled thinking. His death was the outcome of fragmented thought, the result of the activity of the collective egos of different groups of people who were determined to ensure that their self-centred interests were preserved and their identities maintained. We have discussed at length the relationship between ego and "non-being" and how this leads to fragmented thought and activity that we describe as evil. When this happens cognizance of spiritual reality is lost and, what's more, the problem becomes exacerbated in situations of a collective nature which promote mob rule.

It is a fact that evil exists, an outcome of "non-being", a negative aspect of reality born of ignorance which we have to confront in life through the power of the 'courage to be'. The concept of an omnipotent, omniscient entity that is able to intervene directly to influence events in this world leaves a lot of questions to be answered. I feel sure that the universe is ordered by a creative intelligence but I believe that this intelligence manifests itself in subtle ways which cannot always influence events overtly and preclude human suffering.

It would seem that we should be careful about how we interpret myths and the 'truth' that they contain. Hick[9] points out that the Christian myth has proved, over the centuries, to be "powerfully salvific" and asks whether we can continue to live within it whilst being aware of its mythic character. We touched on this subject earlier when we suggested that love is the foundation of the truth of faith and that the actualising of the precept of Jesus, to love one's neighbour as oneself, is the essential feature of the truth of the philosophy of this faith.

When we examine the truth of the myth of traditional Christianity, we see that it is based on a world-view that was relevant two thousand years ago. The Jewish culture at that time perceived God in theistic terms, as a father figure who viewed the world through human eyes because man was created in his own image. He demanded obedience from mankind and when man was disobedient (or sinful) he was dismissed from God's sight, in much the same way as a naughty child may be sent to his bedroom. God was holy and unable to tolerate man's wilful, sinful nature. Before

God was prepared to forgive him for being disobedient he had to be contrite and this display of contrition took the form of appeasement through the process of sacrifice. The concepts of the scapegoat, onto which was loaded man's sin, and the sacrificial lamb of the Passover, were at the forefront of their thinking. It was a natural progression to view Jesus as the "Lamb of God" who died for their sins.

I believe that the myth of traditional Christianity is based on a perception of reality which is no longer tenable to modern man. During the past two millennia, the symbol of the Cross has stood as a central focus for the Christian faith but it has served to represent the sacrifice of God's son. This has portrayed God as a theistic entity rather than the process of Reality. I believe that, for many people today, the cross has ceased to be a meaningful symbol within the myth in its original form, but maybe it can be resurrected and made significant for our present time.

Jesus recognised that his true nature or "being" was grounded in a reality ("Being-itself") from which he could not be separated (we are told that he said, 'I and the Father are one.'). Furthermore he recognised the existence of another side to his nature, his ego, which was a source of distraction (and metaphorically represented by what he called Satan) that turned his attention away from the spiritual dimension which was the path to love, joy and peace. When he talked about dying to our self and being born again, he was talking about killing the ego, that part of our nature which is illusory, so that the spiritual dimension, our real self can be liberated or born again. Using the symbol of the cross, is this not synonymous with crucifying the ego and resurrecting the spirit?

Hick[10] asks whether Christians can be expected to see Jesus, no longer as God incarnate, but as a brother who was far ahead of the rest of us in his openness to God. Equally, one could ask the question, "Are we not all 'sons of God' in terms of the understanding of our real nature or "being" as grounded in "Being-itself"?" Should we not all aspire to a relationship with the "Ground of Being" for which Jesus is a role-model? Is this not a conception of Christianity which is consistent with an up-to-date perception of reality?

Genuine Religiousness

What is the difference between the behaviour of a man who sacrifices his life in an effort to save a fellow human being, and that of an ant which sacrifices itself in defence of its colony?

We have talked about the unconscious having spiritual and instinctual components. The latter is rooted in a genetic, biological predisposition to certain forms of action which seeks to preserve the individual, or the survival of the species, whereas the former is the function of a phenomenon that recognises that our essence is "being" and that this is a universal quality which transcends our individuality. Human beings appear capable of actions which proceed from both sources of unconscious activity, whereas Frankl suggests that other animals appear to be restricted to instinctive reactions, related to environmental signs and signals which are strictly schematic and rigid for each species

It would appear that the activity which prompts self-sacrifice in man is an expression of love and is a function of the intuitive depths of the spiritual unconscious. What Frankl refers to as "intentional feelings" are genuine, heart-felt feelings which arise as a consequence of spiritual love and are a reliable indicator which guides authentic, intuitive action. Emotions which give rise to extreme irrational passion are a function of what Frankl refers to as vital instincts, the 'id' that drives the ego and gives rise to attachment and infatuation.

Frankl[11] suggests that man is conscious of a sense of responsibility which has unconscious spiritual depths, and that he is aware of a relationship which links his immanent self with a reality which appears both immanent and transcendent. The question is: what is the nature of this relationship which man senses with the transcendent, that is linked to the mystery of reality? Frankl views the transcendent unconscious as an existential agent which is part of spiritual existence rather than psychophysical facticity.

If the universe is a sea of energy which appears to manifest intelligence, how does man's form relate to this intelligent source of reality? The religions that developed in the Middle East related to the transcendent in personal terms, through an "I" /"Thou" relationship which was dualistic and anthropocentric. I cannot conceive this relationship in inter-personal terms as I believe that the nature of this reality is formless, unmanifest and beyond the level of man's understanding. I find that Bohm's metaphor, which likens human form to ripples in the stream of reality, is the best way I can conceive our relationship with the transcendent. The idea that our "being" manifests itself through configurations of energy within a sea of energy, to which we experience a sense of connection, seems to me to be a metaphorical interpretation to which I can relate. Any form of communication will be related to an exchange of energy.

If man is sensitive to his spiritual unconscious he will experience a tension between what we have called the essential self, and the ego. The instincts driving his ego will be pushing him away from the "Ground of Being", or fragmenting him from his fellow man, whereas the transcendent unconscious will be drawing him (through his conscience) toward the" Ground of Being" and his fellow man, through the process of love (a spiritual force of gravity).

The transcendent unconscious could be viewed as a constant existential agent (to use Frankl's terminology) that seeks to draw the essence of man's "being" into harmony with the ground of its origin and the "being" of his fellow man. Using an analogy to planetary motion (see Figure 6.1), we could view a planet as the essential self, the sun as the "Ground of Being", love (as a function of the transcendent unconscious) as the force of gravity and ego activity in terms of centrifugal force. The more man is driven by the instincts that drive the ego, the greater the centrifugal force which pushes or drives him further away from the influence of the "Ground of Being". Conversely, the less he is driven by the drives of the ego, the lesser the centrifugal force and the closer he is pulled toward the "Ground of Being". The mystic may well say that, during the course of deep meditation, he has eradicated his ego completely and that his essential self has been drawn into and has merged with the ground of his origin.

```
        Sun              Planet
              Force of Gravity    Centrifugal Force


                          ←    ○    →


                     Love              Ego
     Ground of Being
                         Essential Self
```

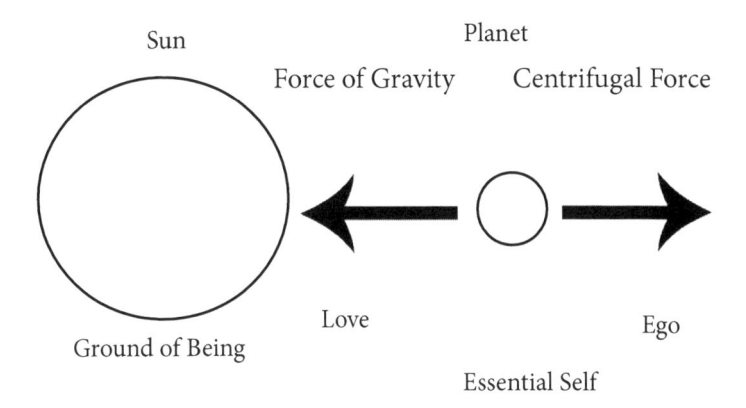

Figure 6.1

There is also a connection between this analogy and the one concerning the electric circuit. A reduction of ego activity leads to decreasing resistance and an increased flow in spiritual energy, with the subsequent production of light and a warm glow. Similarly, a reduction in the centrifugal force of a reduced ego makes the individual more receptive to the transcendent unconscious and subject to the spiritual, gravitational pull of love. This draws him toward the Ground of Being with the subsequent realisation of a sense of unity, wholeness, peace and joy.

It is the spiritual dimension that is the source of ultimate meaning and it seeks to inspire psychophysical expression which operates beyond the influence of the ego. This activity is not driven by the instincts of the 'id', but is pulled gently by the influence of love, to create an environment which is inclusive, non-judgemental and compassionate. It is unconscious religiousness and its source is a transcendent, spiritual agency rather than the process of psychophysical activity operating in isolation.

When man is pulled or drawn by love to act intuitively, in a way which is self-sacrificial, his actions are motivated by a spiritual source, whereas the instinct of the ant to defend the colony is related to genetic programming. Frankl[12] argues that the spiritual and existential character of unconscious religiousness is not of the realm of psychophysical facticity and that we cannot regard it as innate or tied up with heredity, although it stems from the personal centre of the individual man.

It is apparent that Jean Paul Sartre's view of existentialism implied that the universe has no meaning other than that which is conceived by the individual from a psychophysical standpoint. However, if man listens to the voice of his ego and is insensitive to the spiritual unconscious, he is driven by the ego and, like a rocket that breaks free from the gravitational pull of the Earth he becomes lost in space and destined to wander aimlessly.

So what is genuine religiousness? Frankl[13] suggests it is not the result of a religious drive or instinct and belongs to spiritual existence rather than psychophysical activity. It follows from this argument that fundamentalist forms of religion are not genuine, but idolatrous, because they are driven by the collective ego of the participants. They lead to a state of fragmentation, whereas genuine religiousness leads to wholeness and unity.

Something calls each of us to respond to situations in life and it is up to the individual to interpret the nature of this calling. In my eyes, man is influenced by two distinct sources which vie for his attention: the spiritual and the psychological. If man's response is truly spiritual it will be based on the inner conviction that love gives ultimate meaning to human existence. We must not become sidetracked by the issue of dogmatic beliefs which are, in effect, metaphorical conceptions that arise through limited perceptions. Love is the ultimate value leading to a resonance between our sense of "being" and the transcendent ground of its origin and genuine religiousness is founded on this realisation. Any psychophysical form of religion which recognises and acts on this premise is, [in my opinion] genuinely religious.

Beyond Theism

Theological theism promotes a person to person relationship between God and man who have a reality independent of each other. God is perceived as an infinite being who created the world but is separate from his creation. According to the Old Testament He is holy and in conflict with man who is sinful and not worthy enough to set eyes on Him. In this conception, God is perceived as a 'self' with an apparent ego, as a being as opposed to the concept of "Being-itself". He is bound up in a subject-object structure and is portrayed as an invincible autocrat, the being in contrast with whom, all other beings are without freedom. It is this concept of God against which Nietzsche and others rebelled, and to which atheism is opposed.

Eastern religions such as Buddhism, that are not theistic, seek through meditation to transcend the limits of subjectivity and objectivity in an attempt to become one with what Tillich would call the "Ground of Being". According to Tillich, God was not a being but the power that called "being" forth in all creatures, an internal reality which gave meaning to life. One could experience an awareness of the "Ground of Being" within one's relationships with others but any objective definition of this reality was impossible.

Spong[14], like Krishnamurti, asks a challenging question:

"Is the Ground of Being real, or is it a philosophical abstraction serving merely to cushion our awakening into the radical aloneness of living in a godless world?"

Does the dispensing with a personal God mean that the core and ground of all life is impersonal? Surely the answers to this question are revealed within our experience of life. We experience a sense of peace and joy when we reach out to others in a way that recognises our common humanity, our shared "being". The sense of harmony appears to resonate in a way that we intuitively recognise as synchronous with the order of reality. It seems as if our "being" vibrates in unison with that of our fellow man and with the heart of the universe that gives life to all living creatures. Although I cannot perceive this aspect of reality as a separate, individual being, I can sense it as a presence in which I participate and which is all-embracing. This is something that we sense ontologically within the core of our "being", it is not something that is cerebral and can be defined in words.

The feeling of participation in a presence which embraces the whole of creation, a reality that draws us to seek unity with itself, provides us with a focus for living which is of ultimate concern. For life to have real meaning and a sense of purpose there must be an inner commitment to live in a way which acknowledges man's common "being" through love. Love is a function of the process of "being", of 'being in action' and not the product of one who acts. Frankl[15] suggests that there is a danger of making love self-conscious, of making an object of oneself for others to observe or for one's own self-observation. If this happens, the genuine nature of love, as a function of the essential self, vanishes and "being" is turned into being observed by oneself or by others. Loving is then in danger of being "id-ified" or turned into a function of the ego.

It is when the ego has died that we experience a deep sense of peace and find the courage to face the vicissitudes of fate. Perhaps it is a mistake to believe that faith is an option that will lead to an easy life, where God gives us what we want to make us happy and ensures that we have a bright future in the hereafter. Faith is a reality which is practised in the eternal "now", it has nothing to do with an insurance policy which guarantees anything that may, or may not happen in the future when our natural life is over. The experience of history shows that life can indeed be very difficult for the man of faith, as illustrated by men like Jesus or, in more recent times, Dietrich Bonhoeffer in Nazi Germany. It is not easy when your commitment to a principle of love conflicts with your own personal safety and comfort.

The Meaning of Prayer in a World with No External Deity

Spong[16] asks,

"But can we still pray if there is no theistic deity who can respond personally to our prayers?"

Prayer is an attempt by something in the depths of our "being" to commune with the source of life in a search for inspiration to pursue a course of right action which transcends thought. It is an internal dynamic which draws our consciousness into unity with the ground of consciousness, rooted in "Being-itself". In so-doing, it calls us to seek unity with our fellow man through the process of love.

Prayer, whatever its nature, is an experience of the unconscious transcendent which inspires meaning. If "Being-itself" is energy, which gives rise to form and intelligence, and if we are forms, beings of energy, ripples or waves in the vast ocean of energy which is the universe, could it be that prayer is an interactive energy exchange which manifests itself in thoughts and feelings? Human thought has viewed this exchange of energy in terms of an interpersonal relationship, a metaphor for the sense of connection we feel with the universe. It visualised the relationship in terms of man and God, where God was a super-being, all-powerful and all-knowing. It is questionable whether this metaphor, which had meaning in ancient times, is appropriate today.

Whatever the reality is that has given form to our "being", there is no doubt that it is both intelligent, powerful and is inextricably linked to our form. Prayer is a form of communication, whereby human beings can access wisdom through the synchronous linkage of energy fields, leading to intuition which is consistent with love, but how this happens is open to interpretation. I personally believe that it is a mistake to conceive a God who is the master controller of the universe and able to manipulate events like a puppeteer pulling the strings of his puppets. Though this phenomenon may act within the physical and spiritual laws of the universe, it appears unable to intervene directly and prevent natural disasters, accidents or acts which are the outcome of recklessness or evil.

Prayer is not about seeking easy options but a search for the courage to meet the changing circumstances of life that challenge our existence. It is not about ingratiating ourselves with an external deity, or Cosmic Ego, who then panders to the whims of our own ego by granting us favours if we bow down before him and are on our best behaviour. Prayer can never be regarded as a process whereby we can obtain security in the certain knowledge that we shall be protected from the changing fortunes of fate. The idea that a theistic God would, out of choice, protect one person from suffering whilst, at the same time, allow somebody else to suffer greatly, is incongruous with the concepts of omnipotence and love, and [in my opinion] untenable. Prayer recognises that life is fragile, uncertain and may be lost at any moment, but at the same time, it is a form of meditative awareness, an act of faith, acknowledging a sense of order within the universe. It is a process which opens the heart and mind to intuitive insight which facilitates the cause of love and provides access to the 'courage to be'.

Prayer should be what Buddhists refer to as mindfulness, a process which is integrated with everyday living and seeks to maintain a high level of conscious awareness so that we do not live unconsciously from the dictates of the ego.

The Relationship between Ethics and Religious Faith

What are we to make of the codes, rules and laws that shape human behaviour? Clearly codes such as the Ten Commandments were a product of the knowledge and values of the people who created them at that point in time and not the result of the divine revelation of a theistic God. The death of theism has created a vacuum by removing the dogmatic, revelatory, traditional basis of ethics. Man has been left to determine for himself what is of ultimate concern, and how the concrete content of his life, in terms of values and behaviour, reflect that ultimate concern. This has resulted in the sense of guilt, emptiness and meaninglessness that we discussed earlier with all the associated problems of depression, suicide etc. Attempts to escape the effects of meaninglessness have led to a resurgence of religious fundamentalism which seeks to live according to outdated perceptions of reality and adopts unrealistic beliefs.

Harris has pointed to a need to create a response to reality which is based on empiricism and reason. This requires that we recognise the consequences of our own behaviour and how these affect the happiness or suffering of others. Spong appears to hold a similar view when he says that the freedom to be oneself needs to embrace a dialogue with the need to enhance the "being" of others. Such values must come from the depths of our "being" as an authentic response to what is of ultimate concern, a response to what is our true faith. As such, I would argue that ethics is very much linked to a religious perception of what is ultimately important in life. Surely we can only live ethically if we treat other people in the way we would like to be treated ourselves. Such a response to life acknowledges our shared "being", acting like a mirror that enables us to see our own reflection within the "being" of others. It reveals the inauthentic nature of all forms of prejudice by exposing the hypocrisy of judgementalism. Spong[17] says,

"When reason reveals, for example, that skin pigmentation is the result of an adaptive process that enables some people to survive well in climates exposed to the direct rays of the sun,

then prejudice based on skin pigmentation becomes a manifestation of ignorance....When a homosexual orientation is revealed by the development of the science of the brain and its neurochemical processes to be a normal part of the sexual spectrum of human life, a given and not a chosen way of life, then it becomes inhumane to use a person's sexual orientation as the basis for a continuing prejudice.

He goes on to say,[18]

To enhance the being and deepen the life of every human being and to free the love that emanates from each person become part of the ultimate and objective standard for determining proper human behaviour. These are the virtues arising from life itself. They are not external to life or vested in the authority of a being outside of life."

Ethics is a response to life which expresses the concrete content of our ultimate concern, what Tillich would regard as our religious faith. If that concern is truly ultimate then our ethical behaviour will be a manifestation of love which comes from the depth of our "being". Any other motivation of behaviour will be less than ultimate and the subject of an idolatrous faith. Spong[19] believes that the role of the Church is not to judge people but to enhance consciousness, expose ignorance and prejudice and to assist people in plumbing the depths of their "being". I agree with him when he says that God is a presence which calls us into responsibility, into contributing to the well-being of all humanity.

Genuine Religious Faith and the Future

Everyday life for most people is a quest for security in some form or another. We live through ego-consciousness which, by definition, is self-centred and makes us feel as though we are in competition with those around us. Feeling vulnerable, we need to grab our fair share of attention and possessions so that we don't get left behind. This is a view of life that leads to injustice, exploitation, crime, suffering and unhappiness. Religion has sought to remedy the situation but our inability to define reality as it is has resulted in humanity employing a range of imaginative responses. What different religions do say is that there is a need to free ourselves from the toxic effects of the ego and thus become free to love our neighbour who is, in effect, everyone.

Is it possible to replace religious pluralism by religious universalism or is the question paradoxical? If our religion is to be genuine, it has to be our heart-felt response to life in the moment which is intuitive and cannot be defined in words. If religion is such a personal response to life, and defies prescription, how can it be defined universally? The universal definition of religion must be 'Love in Action' and this cannot be embodied in any belief system. It has to be the heart-felt intuitive response of the individual to what is needed in the moment.

If religion is such a personal response to life and cannot be defined universally, what hope do we have of creating a world where the spiritual reality of love has a chance to flourish? How do we make the spiritual reality of love into something that can influence and inspire the lives of other people, and create a sense of community which embodies this ultimate value? The only way we can do this is by trying to make this reality transparent in the way we live, by showing, through practical action, the process of love in action and by revealing the peace and joy that are concomitant from such action. People like Jesus or, in more recent times, Mother Theresa, Martin Luther King or Nelson Mandela have inspired countless numbers to examine their lifestyles and values. What they achieved in their lives called for great personal sacrifice, but their commitment to the spiritual imperative of love enabled them to come to terms with their own personal egos. As a consequence, each of them discovered the power of the 'courage to be' which sustained them in their quest to fulfil the role that destiny had placed before them.

Spong[20], a self-confessed Christian exile, offers some thoughts as to how religion may discover new forms of expression which will inspire those people who are searching for a spiritual commitment to living. He suggests,

"Worship beyond the exile will not be oriented toward an external God but toward the world of our human community. That, however, will not result in a shallow humanism but in a recognition that the place where God is ultimately found is in the depths of our own humanity."

There is a need for God to be perceived as a presence at the heart of life, available to everyone and not as the special possession of a religious institution. We must be careful not to give undue emphasis to faith as belief but seek to act in the eternal "now", through intuitive perception which speaks through the heart and with a vitality and conviction that is an authentic manifestation of truth, as it is perceived in the moment. Worship of God would become a practical commitment of service to the human community.

What the world needs is leaders who will recognise this reality and seek to end the fragmentation which divides different nations and cultures. The problem is that political activity is a function of the collective ego and interests of different political groups and its roots are entangled within psychological time. Whilst the majority of human beings remain ignorant of the nature of this phenomenon, the system will continue to operate from the perspective of the interests of those who hold a balance of power. It is difficult to see how this will change in the near future.

We human beings are not all we were created to be and this is because we are trapped in a nature that is a prisoner of its own limits. These limits are the survival instincts of the illusory ego which are a legacy of our evolutionary past. We need to move forward beyond these limits and encounter a reality in which our "being" is grounded and through which we discover our true essential self. Spong[21] says,

"As I am empowered, affirmed and called by the life-giving power of love to venture nearer and nearer to that ultimate core of being, I discover myself shedding limits, abandoning my security walls, and being freed to give more of my life and my being away. Remarkably, this giving experience is not accompanied by any sense of loss. I also discover an ability to accept and even to love what at an earlier and less secure time in my life I could not, or would not have been able even to tolerate."

The above statement illustrates the dynamic relationship between "being" and "non-being". Spong says that the nearer he ventures to his core of "being", the more he discovers an ability (through the power of love) to shed the limitations of his ego. By drawing closer to the "Ground of Being" he is living in a more conscious way, reducing the resistance of ego in the circuit of his life. He then experiences the increase in his power to love which flows abundantly. Consequently, as the influence of ego diminishes, he discovers a greater level of tolerance and security because he is not caught in psychological time and preoccupied with his illusory self.

It seems to me that any truly spiritual way forward in the future must be grounded in the foremost acceptance of the reality of shared "being". This conviction needs to be allied to a heart-felt approach to living which responds intuitively to life experience in an attempt to avoid the pitfalls of psychological time. This clearly involves a change of mind-set which is mind-blowing in so far as it recognises the limitations of brain-initiated thought which can be locked in psychological time.

Spiritual development may then be seen to be a process which attempts to extricate us from the web of psychological time. Life becomes influenced by mindfulness, whereby we live in a way in which we are more conscious or mindful of our true nature and learn to recognise the illusory influence of the ego.

Finally, Spong[22] says,

"I also assert that making it possible for everyone else to live, to love, and to be is the only mission that Christian people possess. Our task is not to convert; our task is to call people into the depths of their own capacity to be."

I suspect that this statement will strike a chord that will resonate within the hearts of most people, and may provide a focus for genuine religious activity that crosses cultural boundaries and is not defined by dogmatic belief. If religion is to be genuine it has to be a heart-felt response to life as it is perceived in the moment. It cannot be based on dogma that is rigid and inflexible, and inconsistent with our changing perceptions of reality.

Summary of Key Ideas

- Language developed as a tool to enable man to interpret manifest reality which has physical referents. It is unable to define unmanifest reality which is timeless and has no physical referent.
- Ultimate Reality, or God, is beyond human conception and can only be alluded to in a metaphorical poetic way. Different religions are different conceptions of ultimate reality which have found expression in different cultural settings.
- Myths make use of metaphorical language, they are attempts to express perceived truths about reality that are difficult to express literally.
- Genuine religiousness is founded on the realisation that love is the essential value which gives ultimate meaning to human existence. Any psychophysical form of religion which recognises and acts on this premise is,[in my opinion] genuinely religious.
- Faith is an activity which is practised in the eternal "now" and has nothing to do with an insurance policy which guarantees anything that may, or may not happen in the future.
- Prayer is an internal process which draws our consciousness into unity with the ground of consciousness, rooted in "Being-itself". Whatever its nature, it is an experience of the unconscious transcendent which inspires meaning.
- Prayer is not about seeking easy options but a search for the courage to meet the changing circumstances of life that challenge our existence.

- Ethics is a response to life which is consistent with the values that define what is of ultimate concern to the individual. This could be viewed as an expression of one's religious faith. Authentic ethical behaviour will be a manifestation of love in action, an intuitive response which comes from the heart.
- If our religion is to be genuine it has to be our heartfelt response to life in the moment. This is not something that can be prescribed universally or embodied in any belief system. It must be 'Love in Action', a response to what is needed in the moment.
- Authentic religious practice should be a practical commitment of service to the human community. It should be a process whereby we attempt to relate to each other through the essence of our being.

EPILOGUE.

The Having and Being Modes of Living

We have suggested that genuine religiousness implies a psychophysical approach to living which is rooted in "being" and consistent with the spiritual reality that we call love. Over thirty years ago, the psychologist, social philosopher and author, Dr. Erich Fromm wrote an excellent book entitled: 'To Have or to Be'. He identified and considered two radically different ways of living that relate to "being" and "nonbeing", and which he referred to as the 'Being Mode' and the 'Having Mode'. If religious faith is to have any value it must be related to everyday living. In view of this, I cannot think of a more appropriate way to draw this book to a close than by discussing some of Fromm's thoughts and how they relate to the ideas discussed in this book.

What is the Having Mode?

We live in a society which attaches great importance to the acquisition of private property. Our most prized possession is our ego which encompasses many things: our body, name, self-image, possessions and a mixture of perceived qualities. We have already suggested that the ego is a source of "nonbeing", and whatever comprises the content, our ego is experienced as an entity or thing. When we live in a way which is egocentric we tend to be preoccupied with what we have, what we possess in terms of material objects, knowledge and opinions and this orientation is referred to by Fromm as the 'having mode'.

What is the Being Mode?

Fromm[1] says,

"Having refers to things and things are fixed and describable. Being refers to experience, and human experience is in principle not describable. What is fully describable is our persona – the mask we wear, the ego we present – for this persona is in itself a thing. In contrast, the living human being is not a dead image and cannot be described like a thing.....Only in the process of mutual alive relatedness can the other and I overcome the barrier of separateness... Yet our full identification with each other can never be achieved."

Our senses appear to confirm that existence is of an individual nature which separates us from other people, but this is not perceived ontologically in the depths of our "being". Here we experience a relationship between the essence of our "being" and its ground of origin. This calls us into a relationship with others which seeks to overcome the barrier of separateness.

This is the ultimate concern which lies at the heart and soul of every individual and which seeks expression in that person's everyday life. When the individual strives consciously to make this a reality, they are living in the 'being mode'. There is a resonance between their behaviour and reality, or the 'Ground of Being', and this brings with it a joy to living. Fromm alludes to the fact that no matter how much we try to break down barriers through love we can never fully identify with each other.

"Being" is a form of activity which gives expression to our talents. It cannot be expressed in words, for as we have already shown, there is no reflective correspondence between words and experience. It can only be shared or experienced in the "now" moment.

The Difference between Having and Being

Jesus said, *"For whoever wants to save his life will lose it, but whoever loses his life for me will save it. What good is it for a man to gain the whole world, and yet lose or forfeit his very self? (Luke 9:24-25)*

It seems to me that having is a function of the ego whereas "being" is a function of the soul. People who live through the ego live their lives predominantly in the 'having mode', become too preoccupied with material possessions or other aspects of this orientation, and they lose sight or consciousness of their essential self which is soul-related. Those who live from the perspective of the soul realise that their essential self is grounded in "being" and seek to live their life in the 'being mode'. This involves an authentic relatedness to the world whereby they make productive use of their talents in a way which acknowledges and relates to the "being" in others. They endeavour to set aside the demands of the ego so that they remain conscious of their real identity and so, in other words, they lose their illusory self and find their true essential self. This is what Jesus means when he says, *"whoever loses his life for me will save it."*

We have already considered the use of language with

regard to "being" and noted that we are talking about a process (verb) in contrast to an object (noun). It appears to me significant that the 'having mode' is concerned with possessing 'things' (nouns) whereas the 'being mode' is more concerned with productive activity (verb).

Having and "being" are two modes of existence, two different kinds of orientation towards self and the world, the respective dominance of which determines the totality of a person's thinking, feeling and behaviour. In the 'having mode' of existence I want to make things, people and knowledge my property. In the 'being mode' I want to have an authentic relatedness to the world.

Having and Being in the Daily Experience of Life

Learning

Learning in the 'having mode' is concerned with acquisition of knowledge or statements by rote learning. Fromm[2] says,

"Indeed, to one for whom having is the main form of relatedness to the world, ideas that cannot easily be pinned down (or penned down) are frightening – like everything else that grows and changes, and is not controllable."

By contrast, people in the 'being mode' listen to ideas and respond to them in a productive way. Their thinking processes are stimulated and new perspectives arise in their minds. They do not simply acquire knowledge but their cognitive structures change and adapt to new ideas. It seems to me that any fundamentalist thinking is connected to the 'having mode' of knowledge which is unable to adapt to the changing nature of reality.

Conversing

Fromm[3] suggests that when people in the 'having mode' converse they tend to identify with their own opinions which they view as possessions. They do not listen actively, and each is either concerned with impressing the other, or defending his point of view (they act from the ego). Any change of opinion would be viewed as a lost possession, a loss of face or impoverishment.

However, people who converse in the 'being mode' respond spontaneously, productively and generate new ideas because they are not holding on to anything. They are not concerned about bolstering their egos. The "being" persons, in contrast to the "having" persons who rely on what they have, rejoice in the fact that they are, they come alive in the conversation because they are open to new ideas and not anxiously concerned with defending their opinions. Their openness helps others to transcend their egocentricity and who is right or wrong isn't the main issue.

Having Knowledge and Knowing

Fromm says[4],

*"The difference between the mode of having and the mode of being in the sphere of **knowing** is expressed in two formulations: 'I have knowledge' and 'I know'. **Having** knowledge is taking and keeping possession of available knowledge or information; **knowing** is functional and part of the process of productive thinking."*

We have already discussed the fact that our picture of reality does not correspond to what is 'really real' and that most people are unaware of the fact that much of what they hold to be true and self-evident is illusion, produced by the suggestive influence of their environment. Fromm says,

"Knowing begins with the shattering of illusions....Knowing means to penetrate through the surface, in order to arrive at the roots, and hence the causes; knowing means to 'see' reality in its nakedness. Knowing does not mean to be in possession of the truth; it means to penetrate the surface and to strive critically and actively in order to approach truth ever more closely."

This is consistent with what we said earlier about the lack of reflective correspondence between the content of thought with 'real things'. Knowing is not an absolute process, it is an active striving (part of the process of "being") to create conceptual models which relate ever more closely to our changing perception of reality, or, as Fromm says, *"...to approach truth ever more closely."*

Fromm[5] says,

"Optimum knowledge in the being mode is to know more deeply. In the having mode it is to have more knowledge."

Master Eckhart said that man ought to be empty of his own knowledge. Fromm[6] explains that this does not mean that one should forget what one knows, but rather one should forget that one knows. This is to say that we should not look at our knowledge as a possession, in which we find security and which gives us a sense of identity. Knowledge should not assume the form of dogma which binds us as it does in the' having (fundamentalist) mode'. It should, in the 'being mode', be a penetrating activity of thought, an evolutionary process that is alive and does not stand still.

Loving

Fromm[7] asks,

"Can one have love? If we could, love would need to be a thing, a substance that one can have, own, possess. The truth is, there is no such thing as 'love'. ....In reality, there exists only the act of loving. To love is a productive activity. It implies caring for, knowing, responding, affirming, enjoying: the person, the tree, the painting, the idea. It means bringing to life, increasing his/her/its aliveness. It is a process, self-renewing and self-increasing."

We have established that "being" is an active, vital process that is the essence of who we are. We suggested earlier that love was an active response to the "being" in others that is life-enhancing and recognises and values that essence as what is of ultimate value. It implies that we show to others a degree of care and concern that we would like to receive from them.

However, love experienced in the mode of having perceives that which is loved as an object to be possessed and controlled. This subject/object duality is symptomatic of the activity of the ego, it is not life-giving but suffocating, and is a misuse of the word love.

The Will to Give, to Share, to Sacrifice

When discussing the modes of 'having' and "being", Fromm[8] says,

".....both tendencies are present in human beings: the one, to have – to possess – that owes its strength in the last analysis to the biological factor of the desire for survival; the other, to

be – to share, to give, to sacrifice – that owes its strength to the specific conditions of human existence and the inherent need to overcome one's isolation by oneness with others. From these two contradictory strivings in every human being it follows that the social structure, its values and norms, decides which of the two become dominant."

A basic human instinct is that of survival and man uses his cognitive and mechanical functions to the best of his ability to ensure the survival of his biological organism. He needs to provide for his basic needs of food, water, clothing, and shelter from the elements, and this he has done since his arrival on the planet. Throughout history, his understanding of his environment and the raw materials which it contains has evolved, under the influence of creative intelligence, to such an extent that he is more than able to meet these requirements. As we have already suggested, technological development has progressed to such a degree that man has learned to create artificial needs.

The advertising industry goes to great lengths to convince him that certain items are necessities which he needs to acquire in order to be desirable and sexy. Life has become dominated by the demands of the ego and what was initially a quest for biological survival has been replaced by an unhealthy preoccupation with the needs and the survival of the ego. It is a sad indictment of modern-day living that, in spite of technological progress, there are large numbers of people in the world who do not have access to what are truly the basic necessities of life and they struggle to avoid starvation.

It would seem that our ability to share, to give or to empathise with the plight of those who are deprived has been inhibited (i.e., that the 'having mode' of living has become dominant in suppressing our ability to live in the 'being mode'). As Fromm says, these are two contradictory strivings and it is clear which of the two is dominant in the modern era: the dynamic has moved in the direction of nonbeing or the having mode.

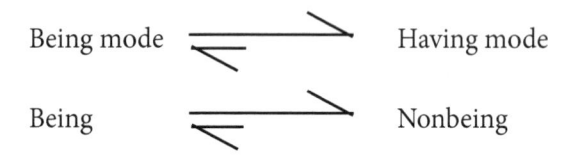

Being mode ⇌ Having mode

Being ⇌ Nonbeing

It is clear that modern culture is fostering the greed for possession, and equally clear that many people are uneasy about the situation and would like to do something about it. However, Fromm, who was a psychoanalyst, was conscious of a paradox within the human condition whereby individuals, who in the depth of their "being" are drawn toward compassion, do not like to be different and buck the trend. It seems to me as though there is a complex, dynamic interaction of competing feelings and thoughts, that originate from both cognitive and spiritual sources that relate to the dynamic between "being" and "nonbeing".

I believe that most people are conscious of an inner need to be at one with each other, and that this need echoes within the cognitive structures of the mind as it tries to make sense of reality. However, as we have already discussed, fragmentation of thought results in the misperception of reality. Man tends to focus on his individuality, from the perspective of an ego which is fragile, insecure and causes him to experience different forms of anxiety. It searches for security in the company of like-minded individuals who share the same ideas and values. It seeks a pseudo form of 'love' or unity which it has lost in the depths of its "being".

Consequently, individuals pursue lifestyles defined by the thoughts and values of the groups to which they subscribe. They are aware of the inequalities of life, are moved to feel compassion at the suffering that they witness on their television screen but do little to change the status quo. They appear to be bound by a state of inertia which inhibits their capability to respond to situations that could be resolved. It seems to me that most people, in the depths of their "being", are compassionate and possess an inner desire to respond to the misfortune of their fellow man but are reluctant to act in isolation. If, in the event of a disaster taking place somewhere in the world, the government was to impose a tax of £1 per person, in order to provide relief for those people involved, would not the majority be prepared to pay that tax?

There appears to be an unwillingness to act unilaterally, people are happy to share a burden but do not feel that they should do more than their fair share. Why should they do something when many do nothing? Fromm points out that we have developed a society whose principles of acquisition, profit, and property have produced a social character oriented around having and, once this dominant pattern is established, nobody wants to be an outsider or be different. Why is it that it takes the extreme conditions of wartime to induce man to forget his self-centred disposition, to lift him from the inertia of "nonbeing" and to act in a unified way for the benefit of the common good? I suspect that when he is faced with extreme situations, man becomes conscious of what really matters, of a concern that transcends his individual ego. He becomes aware of shared "being" or love which compels him to make sacrifices through the power of the 'courage to be'.

Security/Insecurity

People who live in the having mode look for security in what they have: money, possessions, image etc. They become obsessed with these issues and, like a drowning man who thrashes around in the water, desperately trying to stay afloat, they strive hard to cling on to them at all cost, for to lose them would be to lose their sense of identity. They do not realise that if they were to relax and let go they would float to the surface. If they were to let go of the concerns of the ego, the 'having mode' of living, then they would discover a new dimension to life which is rooted in their essential self and "being".

However, the anxiety and insecurity that is created through the danger of losing what one has, does not apply to the 'being mode'. If I am who I am and not what I have, nobody can threaten my security or sense of identity, for my capacity for "being" is essentially, who I am. This, of course, becomes less straightforward in extreme situations such as incapacitating illness or torture but, even then, people have shown amazing fortitude in facing the most challenging situations, strengthened by the 'courage to be'. The only threat to security in "being" lies in a lack of self-belief, a lack of faith in life as expressed through an ultimate concern.

It should be clear that there is no such thing as security as none of us know what fate has in store for us. All that can really be said is that he, whose ultimate concern is rooted in the union of his "being" with "Being-itself", will find access to the 'courage to be' which will provide him with the strength to deal with whatever life brings his way.

Sin and Forgiveness

In Biblical times, sin was conceived to be disobedience to God's will, which is not surprising for, as we have already discussed, God was conceived of as a patriarchal authority figure. This was later translated into disobedience of the moral and religious authority of the Church.

Fromm[9] says,

"Sin in the conventional theological and secular sense is a concept within the authoritarian structure, and this structure belongs to the having mode of existence. Our human centre does not lie in ourselves, but in the authority to which we submit. We do not arrive at well-being by our own productive activity, but by passive obedience, and the ensuing approval by the authority. We have a leader (secular or spiritual, king/queen or God) in whom we have faith; we <u>have</u> security...as long as we <u>are</u>... nobody."

Fromm implies that we live in the mode of "having" to the extent that we internalise the authoritarian structure of our society. We may not necessarily be conscious of this submission and it may be mild or severe. Here we can see how inauthentic guilt relates to misplaced deference toward an ego (or the collective ego of a religious or political group) which is authoritarian and seeks to control.

If sin, as disobedience, is a conception rooted in the 'having mode', what is the meaning of sin in the 'being mode'? We have already considered this in principle, it is the sense of separation felt when the individual is cut off from the power of "Being-itself" or from the "being" of his fellow man. It is the feeling of estrangement when love is absent, a feeling that can lead to the experience of authentic guilt which is resolved by the manifestation of love.

Being and the Eternal Now

The mode of "being" exists only in the here and now, whereas the mode of "having" exists in the past, present and future. When we operate in the 'being mode' we are completely involved in what we are doing, our attention or awareness is fully focused on the activity whether this be creative or otherwise. What we are doing takes place in time, but we are so absorbed in the "now" moment that we do not become cognizant of the passage of time.

Acts of creativity appear to transcend the mind because they find their origin in unmanifest reality which is a timeless domain. We often talk of sportsmen 'being in the 'flow'' when they are at the top of their game. When this happens they experience a state whereby they respond automatically to situations as they unfold, without having to consciously think about what they are doing. It is as if they are on 'automatic pilot'. When we operate in the 'being mode' it seems our behaviour is spontaneous, and its origin comes from a source that is not dependant on the function of the brain-dominated mind. The experiences of love, joy and creative insight appear to be timeless and are experienced in the "now" moment. This does not imply that brain-related thought is unnecessary or does not have a place. There are times when we need to use our brain to provide structure to our lives.

Fromm suggests that the reason we experience the concept of time (i.e. past, present and future) is related to the fact that we have a body which exists for a limited period before it dies. We have to sustain the life of this body and this requires a degree of organisation which responds to the different patterns and rhythms of life. There is thus a requirement to recognise and respect a need for the organisation of time if we wish to function effectively within the real world. However, modern industrial man has become dominated by this concept which now rules both his working hours and leisure time. He needs to regain a sense of perspective and release himself from the straitjacket of time in which he is bound. He needs to become more aware of how his ego exerts an irrational influence and learn to recognise and balance its effect with heart-felt intuition.

It is true that many will feel trapped in jobs where unrealistic demands are placed on them by their immediate boss, who in turn feels subjected to unrealistic pressures placed on him, or her. The competitive mind-set that dominates all forms of business, and leads to fragmentation, is a sickness that is born of greed which has a very destructive influence on the way life is lived. Many will feel caught up in a way of life that is not of their choosing, and will feel helpless and unable to do anything about it. If they complain about workload or refuse to comply with unrealistic demands, they feel as though they are damaging their career prospects or risk losing their job. This creates anxiety about how they would pay the mortgage or make ends meet.

Life is not straightforward and man needs to ask himself what he is doing and whether this truly reflects who he is. He needs to make provision for his material needs but must keep a sense of perspective. The pursuit of material possessions can become an unconditional concern, an end in itself that takes control, and he must be careful not to allow his life to ebb away without giving expression to his essential self. The solution lies in his hands and is rooted in faith as ultimate concern.

GLOSSARY

Atheism	Disbelief in the existence of a theistic God (i.e. an external, personal, supernatural, and potentially invasive Being).
Authentic living	The mode of existence outside "psychological time" which accords with a commitment to love as shared "being". It is the attempt to make the spiritual reality of love explicit through psychophysical activity within the context of time and space.
"Being"	The energy that gives life to our form. The essence of living forms.
"Being-itself"	The source of "being"
Empty mind	The silent sense of presence that exists when the mind is still outside of "psychological time".
Essential Self	The 'selfless self'. The personality operating from the perspective of our essence as "being" or through soul

	awareness outside of psychological time
"Ground of Being"	"Being-itself" the source of all "being" within the universal flux.
Inauthentic living	The mode of existence which occurs within "psychological time" when cognizance of spiritual "being" is lost. Life is lived from the perspective of subject/object duality under the influence of the ego.
Metaphysical	Concern about the fundamental principles of existence in terms of substance, time, space, being and knowing, etc.
Ontic truth	Factual information that arises from sensual perception that we can try to 'prove' by tangible 'facts'.
Ontological	Relating to the nature of "being". I believe that ontological experience is linked to intuition and defies definition because of its timeless nature.
Paradigm	A theory or frame of reference that gives meaning to our perceptions and can influence the perceptions we make within our environment.

Physical referent	Manifested form to which the physical senses can refer.
Psychological time	Time when thought is trapped in a perception of oneself as a separate entity, leading to subject/object duality ("I"/"Me"). A loss of awareness of one's essence as "being," and of the universal, shared nature of this essence.
Psychophysical	A combination of the physiological and psychological aspects of existence that arise through the activity of our bodily form within the context of time and space.
Rational mind	The word rational means agreeable with reason. However, when I use the term 'rational mind' emphasis is placed on cognizance of the illusory nature of ego. Therefore, 'irrational mind' operates under the influence of psychological time whereas 'rational mind' operates outside of this influence and in accordance with love.
Theism	The belief in an external, personal, supernatural, and potentially invasive Being that we call God.

REFERENCES

Chapter 1. The End of Faith?

[1] Sam Harris, The End of Faith, p.14, Simon and Schuster, London, 2006.
[2] John Shelby Spong, Why Christianity Must Change or Die, p. 19, HarperCollins, San Francisco, 1999.
[3] Ibid., p.46.
[4] Harris, op. cit., p. 35.
[5] Harris, op. cit., p. 173.
[6] Harris, op. cit., p. 170.
[7] Harris, op. cit., p. 214
[8] Harris, op. cit., p. 219, 221.
[9] Harris, op. cit., p. 65.

Chapter 2. The Mystery of Reality

[1] Stephen R. Covey, The Seven Habits of Highly Effective People, p.24, Simon & Schuster Ltd., London, 1992.
[2] Lynn McTaggart, The Field, p. XV, Element, HarperCollins, London, 2001.
[3] David Bohm, Wholeness and the Implicate Order, p. 61, Routledge Classics, London New York, 2002.
[4] Ibid., p. 14.
[5] Ibid., p.7.
[6] Ibid., p. 63.

[7] Ibid., p. 65.
[8] Ibid., p. 67.
[9] Ibid., p. 69 .
[10] Ibid., p. 70.
[11] Ibid., p. 71.
[12] Ibid., p. 80.
[13] Harris, op. cit., p. 183.
[14] Bohm, op. cit., p. 79.
[15] Deepak Chopra, How to Know God, p. 1, Rider, London, 2001.
[16] Chopra, op. cit., p. 209.
[17] Chopra, op. cit., p. 234.
[18] Chopra, op. cit., p. 212.
[19] Bohm, op. cit., p. 20.
[20] Bohm, op. cit., p. 25.
[21] Bohm, op. cit., p. 27.
[22] Bohm, op. cit., p. 30.
[23] Bohm, op. cit., p. 30.
[24] Harris, op. cit., p.208
[25] Paul Tillich, The Courage to Be, p. 34, Yale University Press, USA, 2000.

Chapter 3. Psychological Time

[1] J. Krishnamurti & David Bohm, The Ending of Time, p.19, HarperCollins, New York, 1985.
[2] David Bohm, Wholeness and the Implicate Order, p.69, Routledge and Kegan Paul, London, New York, 2002.
[3] Krishnamurti & Bohm, op. cit., p.18.
[4] Krishnamurti & Bohm, op. cit., p. 37.
[5] Krishnamurti & Bohm, op. cit., p.225.

[6] Krishnamurti & Bohm, op. cit., p. 226.
[7] Erich Fromm, The Art of Loving, p. 53, Harpercollins, London, 1957.
[8] Krishnamurti & Bohm, op. cit.,p. 261
[9] Krishnamurti & Bohm, op. cit.,p. 263.

Chapter 4. The Nature of Faith

[1] Paul Tillich, Dynamics of Faith, p. 1, HarperCollins, New York, 1958.
[2] Ibid., p. 92.
[3] Ibid., p. 100
[4] Ibid., p. 103.
[5] Ibid., p.132.

Chapter 5. The Courage to be Oneself

[1] Julian Baggini, The Ego Trick, p.7, Granta Publications, London, 2011.
[2] Ibid., p.123.
[3] Paul Tillich, The Courage to Be, p. 80, Yale University Press, USA, 1952.
[4] Ibid., p. 38.
[5] Alan Watts, The Wisdom of Insecurity, p.83, Rider, London, 1997
[6] Ibid., p. 88.
[7] Tillich, Op. cit., p. 46.
[8] Tillich, Op. cit., p. 47
[9] Viktor E. Frankl., Man's Search for Ultimate Meaning, p. 84, Rider, 2011.
[10] Frankl, Ibid., p. 122.

[11] Frankl, Ibid., p. 127.
[12] Frankl, Ibid., p.143.
[13] Frankl, Ibid., p. 134.
[14] Tillich. Op. cit., P. 174.
[15] Tillich, Op. cit., p. 172.
[16] Tillich, Op. cit., p. 89.
[17] Tillich, Op. cit., p. 84.

Chapter 6. The Nature of Genuine Religiousness and the Future of Religion

[1] John Hick, The Fifth Dimension, p. 5, Oneworld, Oxford, 1999.
[2] Ibid., p. 41.
[3] Ibid., p. 32.
[4] Ibid., p. 37.
[5] Ibid., p. 137.
[6] John Shelby Spong, Why Christianity Must Change or Die, p. 90, Harper Collins, San Francisco, 1999.
[7] Ibid., p. 97.
[8] Hick, Op. cit., p. 231.
[9] Hick, Op. cit., p. 237
[10] Hick, Op. cit., p. 239.
[11] Viktor E. Frankl, Man's Search For Ultimate Meaning, p. 67, Rider, 2011.
[12] Frankl, Ibid., p. 72.
[13] Frankl, Ibid., p.71.
[14] Spong, Op. cit., p. 67.
[15] Frankl, Op. cit., p. 53.
[16] Spong, Op. cit., p. 135.
[17] Spong, Op. cit., P. 161.

[18] Spong, Op. cit., p. 162
[19] Spong, Op. cit., p. 166.
[20] Spong, Op. cit., p. 187.
[21] Spong, Op. cit., p. 216.
[22] Spong, Op. cit., p. 218.

Epilogue. The Having and Being Modes of Living

[1] Erich Fromm, To Have or To Be, p.91, Abacus, London, 1978.
[2] Ibid., p. 38.
[3] Ibid., p. 42.
[4] Ibid., p. 47.
[5] Ibid., p. 48.
[6] Ibid., p. 67.
[7] Ibid., p. 52.
[8] Ibid., p. 108.
[9] Ibid., p. 122.

BIBLIOGRAPHY

Baggini, Julian, The Ego Trick, (London, Granta Publications, 2011)

Bohm, David, Wholeness and the Implicate Order,(London, New York, Routledge Classics, 2002)

Chopra, Deepak, How to Know God,(London, Rider, 2001)

Drury, Nevill, The Visionary Human, (Great Britain, Element, 1991)

Fromm, Erich, To Have or To Be, (London, Abacus, 1978)

Fromm, Erich, The Art of Loving, (London, Mandala, 1985)

Fromm, Erich, The Art of Being, (London, Constable, 1993)

Harris, Sam, The End of Faith, (London, Simon and Schuster, 2006)

Hick, John, The Fifth Dimension, (Oxford, Oneworld, 1999)

Krishnamurti, J., & Bohm, D., The Ending of Time, (New York, HarperCollins, 1985)

McTaggart, Lynn, The Field, (London, Harpercollins, 2001)

Spong, John Shelby, Why Christianity Must Change or Die, (San Francisco, HarperCollins, 1999)

Tillich, Paul, The Courage To Be, (USA, Yale University Press, 2000)

Tillich, Paul, Dynamics of Faith, (New York, HarperCollins, 1958)

Tolle, Eckhart, The Power of Now,

Tolle, Eckhart, A New earth, (London, Penguin, 2005)

Watts, Alan, The Wisdom of Insecurity, (London, Rider, 1997)

INDEX

Anxiety, 81, 123-128, 140, 141, 146, 151, 152, 156, 202, 204, 207; of fate and death, 128-133; of emptiness and meaninglessness, 133-136; of guilt and condemnation, 136, 137

Atheism, 2, 181

Atman, 166

Authenticity/inauthenticity, 43, 71- 73, 82, 84, 88, 93, 98, 99, 106, 107, 109, 115-117, 119, 125, 130, 135, 138-140, 143, 145, 149, 152, 161, 177, 186, 189, 196, 197; authentic relationships, 93

Baggini, Julian, 115, 116, 119

"Being": 4, 32, 33, 48, 51-62, 67-69, 72, 74-83, 90-93, 96, 98, 101, 103, 106, 109-111, 115-117, 119, 121-129, 133, 137, 141, 144, 145, 149, 151, 153, 155, 156, 160, 161, 166-170, 175-178, 181, 182, 186, 187, 190, 191, 194-198, 200, 202-206; being-mode of existence, 69, 76, 124, 125, 127, 131, 191-208; 'power of being', 148, 151; pre-logical understanding of "being", 137, 143, 144

"Being-itself" ("Ground of Being"): 4, 32, 41, 48, 51-58, 60, 70, 72, 74, 81, 82, 90, 91, 93, 96, 98, 109-111, 120-122, 124,

128, 129, 132, 133, 141-146, 149, 153, 156, 160, 161, 166-171, 175-182, 184, 190, 195, 205, 206; 'power of Being-itself' (Holy Spirit?), 148, 151, 172; 'Will to be', the, 155

Beliefs, 4, 10

Bohm, David, 16- 28, 30, 33, 41-47, 78, 83, 177

Brahman, 166

Buddha, 61, 104, 162; Buddhism, 9, 181, 185

Chopra, Deepak, 33, 34, 36, 37, 49

Christianity, 1, 108, 109, 167, 170-176

Chronological time, 68

Cleverness, 84

Cognitive limitations, 164-166

Concepts, 21, 22, 35, 37-40, 43, 44, 57, 99-101, 106, 107, 111, 144, 160, 161, 164, 165, 199; concepts as configurations of energy, 24-26

Conscience, 137-141, 178; pseudo conscience, 139, 140

Consciousness, 6, 38, 52, 53, 55, 66, 67, 74, 117, 118, 122, 128, 184; altered states of consciousness, 164; the selflessness of consciousness,(see also selfless self) 6-9, 62-64

Conversing in the modes of 'being' and 'having', 198

Courage, 132, 152-157; the 'courage to be', 82, 133, 140, 149, 155-157, 172-174, 185, 189, 204, 205; 'courage of despair', 148

Creativity, 37, 40, 50, 57, 133, 206; creative intelligence, 39-41, 48-50, 70, 72, 73, 83, 85, 120, 122, 174, 201

Despair, 56, 88, 136, 145-149

Doubt, 137, 147

Duality, subject/object, 5-9, 66-69, 77, 81, 90, 93, 94, 130, 177, 181, 184, 200

Eckhart, Master, 81, 199

Ego (see also 'phantom self'/'Separate I'), 3, 4, 9, 41, 46, 55, 60-62, 66-85, 89, 91, 93, 94, 96, 97, 109, 110, 123-127, 129, 133, 136, 137, 139-142, 146, 147, 149, 152, 153, 155, 156, 160-162, 166-168, 172, 173, 175, 177-183, 185, 187-191, 194-196, 198, 200, 201, 204, 205, 207; ego death, 121, 122; collective ego,9, 135, 154, 180, 190, 205

Emptiness, 133, 134, 186

Energy, 14-19, 21-29, 32-37,39, 40, 50-57, 60, 73, 74, 90, 92, 95, 120, 122, 126, 127, 130, 136-138, 142, 144, 150, 161, 177, 178, 184

Estrangement, 62, 96- 98, 111, 138, 139, 141, 156, 206

Ethics, 5, 185-187

Evil, 55, 94, 132, 173, 174, 184

Evolution, 2, 3, 25-31, 37, 39, 40, 50, 57, 70, 75, 77, 79, 98, 101-104, 107, 118, 133, 135, 164, 168, 190, 199, 201

Existential vacuum, 88, 143, 144, 146

Faith: as dogmatic belief, 10; absolute faith, 126; certainty of faith, 111, 112; faith and courage, 111, 112; faith and doubt, 104, 105, 111, 112; faith and ethics, 186, 187; faith and reason, 95-99, 103; faith and love, 109-111; faith in relation to historical truth, 103, 104; faith as 'ultimate concern', 10, 87-91, 95, 96, 98, 99, 103, 105-109, 133, 134, 140, 148, 149, 152, 153, 186, 187, 195, 204, 208; idolatrous faith, 87-91, 134, 140, 144, 154, 180, 187; the philosophy of faith, 105-109; the truth of faith, 105-109

Fear, 123-128, 151; fear of death, 129; fear of suffering, 130-133

Feelings, 37, 53, 54, 89, 113, 114

Fifth dimension, 163

Forgiveness, 141, 142

Fragmentation, 18, 93, 163, 180 189, 207

Frankl, Viktor, 88, 91, 143-145, 147, 176-178, 180, 182

Freedom, 140, 150

Free will, 122, 123

Fromm, Erich, 80, 194-208

Genetic make-up, 120, 121,; Genetic pre-disposition to survival, 75-77, 161, 176, 180

God, 2-6, 15, 30, 32, 90, 101,142, 151, 160-163, 167, 169-176, 181-184, 187, 189

Guilt, 94, 136-143, 186; authentic and inauthentic guilt, 138-141, 205, 206

Harris, Sam, 1-10, 29, 52, 99, 186

Having-mode of existence, 76, 194-208

Heidegger, Martin, 149

Hick, John, 162-166, 169, 170, 174, 176

Hinduism, 166, 167

Hume, 8

Insight, 20, 22, 46, 48, 54, 70

Instinctuality, unconscious, 92, 138, 139, 141, 176-180

Intelligence, 22, 23, 83, 84, 95, 122, 177, 184; intelligence as a form of energy, 22, 23; intelligent perception, 22-24, 29, 35, 39, 48, 69

Intuition, 5, 29, 32, 37, 39, 44, 53-55, 70-74, 75, 83-85, 94, 97, 105, 106, 116, 120, 122, 124, 135, 137, 138, 140, 143, 144, 161, 165, 177, 180, 184, 185, 188, 189, 191, 207

Islam, 1, 154

Jesus, 3, 104, 111, 170-176, 183, 196

Judaism, 1, 109, 170

Julian of Norwich, 167, 168

Knowledge, as an ever-changing art form, 28; knowledge/knowing in the modes of 'being' and 'having', 198, 199

Learning in the modes of 'being' and 'having', 197

Krishnamurti, Jiddu, 66, 73, 83, 85, 182

Love, 32, 33, 45, 48, 72, 74, 79-85, 89, 93, 94, 98, 99, 104, 107, 108-111, 121, 122, 127, 129, 132-135, 137-141, 145, 147, 149, 152, 153, 155, 156, 162, 169-185, 187-191, 194, 200, 204, 206; love as ultimate meaning, 132, 145, 149, 169; Love of God, 143; pseudo love, 147, 203; 'Will to love', the, 155; loving in the modes of 'being' and 'having', 200

Matter, 16-24, 35

McTaggart, Lynn, 14, 15, 19, 34

Meaning, 29, 47, 92,-94, 103, 105, 121, 133-136, 143-149, 179-182, 184; meaning as 'love in action', 145; meaningful relationships, 93, 94; pre-moral understanding of meaning, 137, 143, 144

Meaninglessness, 57, 88, 102, 133, 134, 144-147, 186; the anxiety of meaninglessness, 133-136, 147

Measure: 44-48; measure as insight, 46

Memory, 33, 35

Metaphor, 17, 19, 31, 51, 52, 58-62, 163, 169-174, 177, 181, 184; reality as a flowing stream, 16, 31

Mind, 33-37; particular mind, 34-37, 39, 41, 49, 53, 55, 70, 71 73, 76, 79, 83, 122, 124, 128-130, 161; unconscious mind, 92, 176-179; universal mind, 36, 37, 39, 41, 49, 55, 70-73, 84, 85, 124, 128-130, 135, 144, 161

Mindfulness, 95, 185, 191

Mohammed, 3, 154

Moses, 3

Mysticism, 164, 166, 167, 178

Myth, 169-174

Near death experiences (NDE), 128, 129

Non-being, 56-62, 75, 80, 81, 84, 96, 98, 111, 117, 119, 122, 123, 127, 129, 130, 132, 133, 134, 135, 136, 140, 142, 143, 146, 149, 151, 155, 156, 173, 174, 190, 194, 202, 203

Paradigms, 13

Perception, 12-28, 34, 38, 39, 42, 43, 53, 101

Prayer, 183-185

Providence, 156

Psychological time, 62, 66-85, 91, 94, 96, 97, 107, 111, 114

121, 122, 124-127, 130, 131, 134, 135, 142, 143, 146, 147, 151, 154, 156, 160, 190, 191

Psychophysical, the, 91-96, 98, 99, 105-108, 114, 118, 119, 125, 137, 138, 140, 144, 145, 147, 166, 177, 179-181, 194

Reality, thought about, 19, 101; immeasurable reality, 46-48; manifest reality, 26, 36, 101, 163, 177; unmanifest reality, 26, 28, 29, 36, 48, 51, 90, 102, 163, 177, 206

Religion, 1, 29, 160-191; early religious beliefs, 100-102; decline of religion, 108; religious fundamentalism, 1, 4, 104, 105, 136, 180, 186; genuine religiousness, 180, 181, 191, 194; religious pluralism/universalism, 188; unconscious religiousness, 179, 180

Sacrifice, 82, 109, 170, 175, 176, 180

Salvation, 163, 168, 171

Sartre, Jean Paul, 149, 180

Satan, 175

Science and scientific theories, 14-20, 28, 99-103, 165

Security/insecurity, 9, 74, 79, 101, 126, 127, 131, 135, 136, 148, 160, 185, 187, 191, 199, 202, 204

Self, 6-9, 114-123; phantom self/separate 'I'/ego, 6- 9, 44, 66-85, 116, 117, 121, 126, 127, 129-132, 134, 150, 151, 153; selfless self/essential self, 77, 78, 80, 81, 106, 108-110, 116, 117, 122-125, 127, 128, 130-132, 136, 141, 142, 146, 149-151, 160, 162, 167, 172, 173, 178, 183, 190, 196, 204, 208;

self-affirmation, 133, 134, 136, 137, 151, 153, 156; Divine self-affirmation, 150-152; courage to be oneself (see also the 'courage to be'), 107-147

Sin, 162, 167-170, 173-175, 205

Soul, 30, 33, 53, 70-72, 83, 84, 93, 96, 97, 106-108, 120, 130, 146, 153, 155, 170, 195, 196; soul awareness, 55, 61, 70, 73, 74, 93, 95, 119, 120, 122, 124, 130, 137, 138, 140, 146, 156

Spirit: see "being"; spiritual, 91-94, 97, 103, 106, 141, 142; unconscious spirituality, 92-94, 137, 138, 140, 144, 176-180, 184

Spong, John Shelby, 2, 10, 168, 182, 183, 186, 187, 189-191

Suicide bomber, 154, 155

Survival, 75, 76, 127, 132, 190, 201

Tao, 16

Theism, 2-6, 90, 137, 170-175 181, 185, 186

Thought, 19, 38, 39; thought as energy, 21, 33-37; thought and reality, 23-28; fragmented thought, 19, 30, 41-46, 79, 93, 97, 104, 173, 202; rational thought, 69-74, 135; irrational thought, 69-74, 91, 121; thought and theories, 19, 28, 44

Tillich, Paul, 10, 32, 48, 56, 57, 62, 87, 90, 91, 96, 99, 103, 105, 106, 109, *110,* 127-129, 133, 134, 145, 147-149, 151, 153, 154, 156, 181, 187

Truth, 39, 47, 70, 85, 99-109, 162, 165, 166, 169, 170, 171, 173, 174, 189, 199

Understanding, 24, 38, 39

Universal Flux, 16-19, 23, 31, 32, 34, 37, 51-53, 55, 71 73, 74, 95, 115, 116, 120, 150

Values, 47, 91, 106, 133-135, 137, 144, 147, 149, 153, 181, 185, 186, 188, 189, 203: absolute values, 31; values as a form of measurement, 45-48

Virgin birth, 108, 171

Vitality, 57, 152, 153, 189

Watts, Alan, 8, 130, 131, 162

Wisdom, 84, 85, 95, 184; wisdom of the heart (pre-reflective ontological self-understanding), 143, 144